For Raymond and Gwyneth

Training Foreign Language Teachers

CAMBRIDGE TEACHER TRAINING AND DEVELOPMENT
Series Editors: Marion Williams and Tony Wright

This series is designed for all those involved in language teacher training and development: teachers in training, trainers, directors of studies, advisers, teachers of in-service courses and seminars. Its aim is to provide a comprehensive, organised and authoritative resource for language teacher training and development.

*Original Series Editors: Ruth Gairns and Marion Williams

Teach English – A training course for teachers
by Adrian Doff

Trainer's Handbook
Teacher's Workbook

Models and Metaphors in Language Teacher Training –
Loop input and other strategies*
by Tessa Woodward

Training Foreign Language Teachers – A reflective approach
by Michael J. Wallace
This title was prepared with Roger Bowers as series editor.

Literature and Language Teaching – A guide for teachers and trainers*
by Gillian Lazar

Classroom Observation Tasks – A resource book for language teachers and trainers*
by Ruth Wajnryb

Tasks for Language Teachers – A resource book for training and development*
by Martin Parrott

English for the Teacher – A language development course*
by Mary Spratt

Teaching Children English – A training course for teachers of English to children*
by David Vale with Anne Feunteun

A Course in Language Teaching – Practice and theory
by Penny Ur

Looking at Language Classrooms
A teacher development video package

About Language – Tasks for teachers of English
by Scott Thornbury

Action Research for Language Teachers
by Michael J. Wallace

Training Foreign Language Teachers

A reflective approach

Michael J. Wallace

CAMBRIDGE
UNIVERSITY PRESS

PUBLISHED BY THE PRESS SYNDICATE OF THE UNIVERSITY OF CAMBRIDGE
The Pitt Building, Trumpington Street, Cambridge, United Kingdom

CAMBRIDGE UNIVERSITY PRESS
The Edinburgh Building, Cambridge CB2 2RU, UK
40 West 20th Street, New York, NY 10011–4211, USA
10 Stamford Road, Oakleigh, VIC 3166, Australia
Ruiz de Alarcón 13, 28014 Madrid, Spain
Dock House, The Waterfront, Cape Town 8001, South Africa

http://www.cambridge.org

First published 1991
Ninth printing 2001

Library of Congress catalogue card number: 91–28561

British Library Cataloguing in Publication data
Wallace, Michael J.

Training foreign language teachers: a reflective
approach. – (Cambridge teacher training and development).
1. Language teachers. Professional education.
I. Title
407

ISBN 0 521 35636 9 hardback
ISBN 0 521 35654 7 paperback

Transferred to digital printing 2004

GO

Contents

Acknowledgements

The author and publishers are grateful to the authors, publishers and others who have given permission for the use of copyright material.

The table on page 69 from *Analyzing Teaching Behavior* (Addison Wesley, 1970) is reproduced by permission of Ned Flanders; the DOTE Practical Test Report form on pp. 136–7 is reproduced with the permission of the University of Cambridge Local Examinations Syndicate; the Report on Practical Test form for the Diploma in the Teaching of English Across the Curriculum in Multilingual Schools on pp. 138–40 is reproduced with the permission of the RSA Examinations Board.

Thanks

First, I'd like to thank all the M.A. students, too many unfortunately to mention by name, from many different countries, who have discussed the ideas in this book with me over the past five years. This has been a tremendous learning experience for me, and I am deeply in their debt.

Secondly, I am grateful to my colleagues in Moray House College, who have provided such a stimulating environment for developing educational ideas. I am particularly grateful to Gordon Kirk, Principal of Moray House College, and to Margot Cameron-Jones, Head of the Department of Teaching Studies, who first introduced me to the concept of Reflective Practice. Their influence is pervasive in this book. I am also grateful to some of my colleagues from the Scottish Centre for Education Overseas, namely David Carver, Patricia Ahrens and Iain McWilliam, who have also shared many of their thoughts with me; likewise to Paquita McMichael, Head of the Department of Social Science and Social Studies, and Jim Kidd of the Teaching Studies Department. Thanks also to Esther Dunbar, formerly of Basil Paterson College, Edinburgh, to Robin McKenzie, Principal of Basil Paterson's, and to the other tutors past and present of that college who have cooperated in demonstrating Reflective Practice: I am very much in their debt.

Once more, I am grateful to the library staff of Moray House for their unstinting help: in particular to Liz Leitch, Margaret McKay and David Fairgrieve, with a special vote of thanks to Hazel Robertson for her advice and assistance.

I'd also like to record here my appreciation to Roger Bowers for making many helpful suggestions; to Ruth Gairns for her detailed reading of the text – her suggestions have greatly improved the impact of the book; to Annemarie Young of Cambridge University Press for her patience and understanding during the production of the manuscript; and also to Alison Silver for the benefit of her considerable editorial expertise.

Thanks also to Carole Jackson for handling the typing so cheerfully and efficiently. Thanks (as always) to my wife Eileen for her unfailing support.

Introduction

This book has been written to help anyone in the area of foreign language teaching who is engaged in designing, running or taking part in any of the following kinds of professional activities:

1. teacher education courses, especially in developing countries;
2. in-service training programmes;
3. supervision/inspection programmes;
4. advisory programmes for teachers;
5. management and administration posts which involve some element of staff development;
6. professional self-development programmes.

The book should also be of interest to anyone in the area of foreign language teaching who is involved in thinking about the processes by which professional competence is developed and improved.

The ideas and activities suggested here are the outcome of over twenty years' experience in EFL teaching and teacher education. One of the purposes of the book is to provide something very practical, and indeed many of the suggestions and activities could be put into effect immediately. It should, however, be made clear that the purpose of this book is **not** to suggest the specific content of teacher education inputs, nor even to advocate a particular approach to classroom teaching. Experience suggests that most teacher educators are not short of ideas in these areas: and in any case this need is being met in other publications. The larger purpose of this book is to put various activities and inputs **within the framework of a coherent approach to foreign language teacher education.** All too often foreign language teacher education is a series of 'bright ideas' and/or isolated individual initiatives, so that the resulting learning experience for the trainees can be fragmented and even, in the broadest sense, incoherent. If the present book provides some practical suggestions for foreign language teacher education or supervision, and at the same time affords some food for thought about the larger context of teacher education of which such activities could form a meaningful part, then it will have achieved its main objectives.

Please note that, in cases where the sex of the person being referred to is not known, 'she' has been generally used throughout the book.

'Personal review' sections

The idea of these sections is to help you to think about the issues that have been raised in each chapter, and also to help you to personalise what you have read by relating it to your own situation. Most of the topics will be 'open-ended' – there is no one answer to them, because the answers will depend on your response as an individual. Some of the topics will invite group discussion, so that you and some like-minded colleagues or fellow-trainees can perhaps get together and gain the benefit of one another's experience and insights.

1 Teacher education: Some current models

1.1 Overview

It is normal for teaching to be considered as a 'profession' and for teachers to consider themselves as 'professional' people. I suggest that there are indeed advantages to be gained in looking at teaching as a profession among other professions. But what are the implications of this, especially for teacher education and development? How has professional education traditionally been organised? How *should* it be organised? In this chapter, I will consider three different models of professional education and I will suggest that the 'reflective model' is one which combines within it certain strengths which exist only separately in the other two models that will be considered.

1.2 Language teaching and teacher education

The late twentieth century has been called 'the age of communication', and with some justification. The world is very rapidly turning into the 'global village' which has often been predicted. As the pressure to communicate increases, the divisions of language are felt even more keenly. So language teaching, especially of the great world languages, which are seen as international channels of communication, becomes ever more important.

With the explosion in language teaching there has been an increased demand for language teachers and the consequent need to train these teachers. Thus, many of us who started our careers as language teachers find ourselves in the position of being trainers of language teachers, or in some way responsible for the professional development of language teachers. Parallel with this change, there has been the growing feeling that all of us as language teaching professionals can, and even must, take on the responsibility for our own development. Everywhere there are signs that members of the profession are willing to shoulder that responsibility.

This is without doubt a tremendous professional challenge, but also, to many people, a daunting one. Some of us may see ourselves as operating outside our area of expertise, in the domains, perhaps, of specialists in 'education' or in 'the psychology of learning'. Where does one begin?

This book suggests one path towards 'beginning'. It tries to present a coherent framework of ideas for considering foreign language teacher education and development.

It does not pretend to provide a detailed 'how-to-do-it' of practical tips, although it does claim to have very practical outcomes. Without some kind of coherent intellectual framework, practical tips and bright ideas will not necessarily lead to any effective result. This book is therefore concerned, in the first instance, with exploring some fundamental questions on the nature of teaching and teacher training, and *then* to see how the answers to these questions lead naturally to the consideration of certain techniques and approaches. The book does not purport to have invented a revolutionary new approach to teacher education, but rather seeks to present a coherent rationale of current good teacher education practice, which has already been tried and tested in many educational contexts. It is written from the perspective of a language teacher trainer, but part of the argument is just as applicable to teacher development. The distinction made between 'teacher training or education' on the one hand and 'teacher development' on the other is one that has been made by several writers (for example, Edge, 1988). The distinction is that training or education is something that can be presented or managed by *others*; whereas development is something that can be done only by and for *oneself*. Some writers have also gone on to distinguish between 'training' and 'education', but these terms will be used interchangeably in this book.

1.3 A note on the 'Personal reviews'

I will suggest later in this book that one of the crucial factors in the success of learning anything depends on *what the learners themselves bring to the learning situation*. As psychologists studying learning development have discovered, no learning takes place in a vacuum: it is, rather, a matter of how a learner interacts with what is to be learned in a particular situation. Since anyone reading this book, almost by definition, brings to it a wealth of experience derived from their own personal and professional history, the book will attempt to tap into these personal resources by suggesting topics for 'Personal review'. These can be handled on an individual basis, but most would be richer as learning resources if done on a group basis. They may, however, be skipped if you are in a hurry as the text can usually be interpreted without them.

PERSONAL REVIEW

Think of any teacher education programme (or indeed any training programme), however brief, in which you were involved as a trainee. Make two columns on a sheet of paper, and list the STRENGTHS and WEAKNESSES of the programme. If you can, compare your list with those of other colleagues. What are the common features? Where do you disagree? What conclusions might you draw from this about how teacher education should be organised?

1.4 Teaching and other professions

Unless you have been luckier than most people, your 'Personal review' will have thrown up some personal training experiences that were less than satisfactory. Whenever I have asked experienced teachers from a wide variety of countries to do this exercise, complaints have most commonly focussed on the perceived gap between *theory* and *practice*. What is the best way of handling this issue?

I personally feel that one of the most instructive ways of approaching this problem is by stepping outside the narrow confines of our own profession, and comparing and contrasting it with other professions, as has been done, for example, by Barnett, Becher and Cork (1987) in their article 'Models of professional preparation: pharmacy, nursing and teacher education'. When one does this one discovers that the problems of theory and practice are not solely found in teaching, but are of constant concern to almost every profession.

PERSONAL REVIEW

Compare the way that teachers in your country are trained with the training of any other profession that you know about. What are the similarities and differences? Do you think that teacher educators have anything to learn from these other professions?

1.5   Professions and professionalism

What exactly do we mean by referring to someone as a 'professional'? Which occupations are professions and which are not? 'Professional' is one of those terms which has acquired a whole cluster of overlapping meanings. One common distinction occurs when we speak of a professional player of sports or professional artists who do what they do as a way of making a living. These can be contrasted with amateurs, who practise their sport or art for the love of it. In this sense, it's possible to be an 'amateur' and still be very good: you just don't get paid for it. Sometimes, on the other hand, people use the adjective 'professional' to describe something that has been well done, whereas 'an amateur job' is something that has been badly done. 'Professional', and even 'profession', are therefore 'loaded' words sometimes: they can carry value judgements about the worth of the person or activity referred to.

Originally, the word 'profession' had religious overtones as in 'a profession of faith' (a statement of what one believes in); it also had the sense of dedicating oneself to a calling (today we might call it a 'vocation'). Some professions (medicine, for example) have never lost this sense of a special kind of dedication to the welfare of others. Those engaged in a profession also 'professed' to have a knowledge not available to the public at large, but a knowledge that could be of great public use. This specialised knowledge might be based, for example, on scientific discovery: again, medicine is the most obvious example.

Thus, in 'profession' we have a kind of occupation which can only be practised after long and rigorous academic study, which should be well rewarded because of the difficulty in attaining it and the public good it brings, but which is not simply engaged in for profit, because it also carries a sense of public service and personal dedication. Little wonder that many occupations would wish to be called 'professions'! Fortunately, it is not necessary here to take on the invidious task of deciding which occupations should be called professions and which should not. All that has to be said is that any occupation aspiring to the title of 'profession' will claim at least some of these qualities: a basis of scientific knowledge; a period of rigorous study which is formally assessed; a sense of public service; high standards of professional conduct; and the ability to perform some specified demanding and socially useful tasks in a demonstrably competent manner.

1.6   How is professional expertise acquired?

I would like now to return to the basic issues of professional education and training. How do those engaged in the professions (be they lawyers, doctors, teachers, pharmacists, nurses or whatever) develop their professionalism? I would like to suggest that there are currently three major models of professional education which have historically appeared on the scene in the following order:

1. The craft model
2. The applied science model
3. The reflective model

I will describe each of these in turn.

1.7   The craft model

In this model, the wisdom of the profession resides in an experienced professional practitioner: someone who is expert in the practice of the 'craft'. The young trainee learns by imitating the expert's techniques, and by following the expert's instructions and advice. (Hopefully, what the expert *says* and *does* will not be in conflict.) By this process, expertise in the craft is passed on from generation to generation. This is a very simple model and may be represented thus:

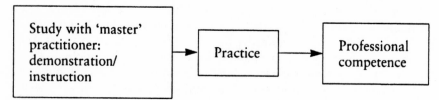

Figure 1.1   The craft model of professional education

According to Stones and Morris (1972:7), this was how teaching practice was traditionally organised until about the end of the Second World War in 1945: 'The *master* teacher told the students what to do, showed them how to do it and the students imitated the master.' Stones and Morris disparagingly categorise this method of professional training as being identical to the system whereby new workers on an assembly line in a factory learned to do routine tasks. This training procedure was called 'sitting with Nellie', Nellie being an experienced worker who had been doing these routine tasks for years.

Stones and Morris rightly point out that this technique is basically conservative and depends, for whatever effectiveness it might have, on an essentially static society. In contemporary society, on the other hand, the one thing we can be sure of is that in ten years' time things will be very different from what they are now. Schools today exist in a dynamic society, geared to change. The concept of the venerable old master teacher is difficult to sustain in an educational context of new methodologies and new syllabuses, where the raw recruit from a College of

Education may be, *in some ways*, better informed than the practising teacher.

Yet the craft model of professional development cannot be dismissed out of hand, and was revived in the mid 1970s by the influential educationalist Lawrence Stenhouse (1975:75). Stenhouse picked up an analogy made by Atkin (1968), in which the latter compares teaching to the craft of metallurgy (making metals). Atkin points out that craftsmen in metallurgy have been successfully making metals for many hundreds of years, with apprentices learning from masters. However, the science of metallurgy has not yet fully succeeded in explaining everything that goes on in this process. Atkin asks whether teaching is not at least as complex as metallurgy.

There is clearly an important truth here, which I will come back to again when I discuss the shortcomings of the 'applied science' model in the next section. Good teaching is an undeniably complex activity, and there is no guarantee that it will ever be fully predictable in a logical way according to 'scientific' principles. On the other hand, the critique which Stones and Morris made of the view of teaching as *primarily* a craft still stands. That view is basically static and does not allow for the explosion of scientific knowledge concerning the very bases of how people think and behave, to say nothing of the tremendous developments in the subject areas which teachers teach. In the case of language teachers, one thinks of the revolutions in the study of linguistics which have taken place in our lifetime, quite apart from the creation and rapid growth of totally new disciplines such as psycholinguistics and sociolinguistics. These considerations bring us naturally on to the view of teaching and other professions as 'applied sciences'.

PERSONAL REVIEW

Before we go on to consider the applied science model, try to reflect on your own position in this question: is teaching a craft or a science? It may help you to consider this question if you take a sheet of paper and make two columns. Put CRAFT and SCIENCE as the headings for the two columns, and under the appropriate heading put those aspects of the profession that you consider 'craft-like' and those you consider 'scientific'. If you are working in a group, how does your list compare with those of other colleagues? What are the implications for teacher education?

1.8 The applied science model

The critique which will be presented here of the 'applied science' and 'reflective' models is basically that put forward by the American sociologist Donald A. Schön in his various writings, notably *The Reflective Practitioner: How Professionals Think in Action* (1983) and his later book *Educating the Reflective Practitioner* (1987). While largely following Schön's critique, I have taken the liberty of substituting what I think are either more transparent or more convenient terms than those used by Schön. His term for what I have here called the 'applied science' model is 'technical rationality', and in the area of what I have called the 'reflective' model he uses a cluster of terms such as 'reflection-in-action,' reflection-on-action,' 'reflective action,' 'reflective practice' and others.

The applied science model is the traditional and probably still the most prevalent model underlying most training or education programmes for the professions, whether they be medicine, architecture, teaching or whatever. This model derives its authority from the achievements of empirical science, particularly in the nineteenth and twentieth centuries. Within this framework practical knowledge of anything is simply a matter of relating the most appropriate means to whatever objectives have been decided on. The whole issue of the practice of a profession is therefore merely *instrumental* in its nature.

It might be helpful at this point to consider some concrete examples from engineering and teaching. In engineering, the objective might be to build a bridge across a gap of a certain width, and capable of bearing a certain load. Using their scientific knowledge of the load bearing and other qualities of various materials, the engineers involved can choose appropriate materials. Using this mathematical/scientific knowledge, they can proceed with the most effective design in terms of the shape and length of the bridge, how it is to be supported and so on.

Many writers on education would analyse teaching problems in a similar way, that is, using scientific knowledge to achieve certain clearly defined objectives. I have already quoted Stones and Morris (1972) who rejected the craft model in favour of a more 'scientific' approach. If the objective is that of maintaining discipline, for example, these authors point out that: 'the important area of classroom and group management has received detailed empirical study, and a body of theoretical and practical knowledge has been amassed which begins to put the problems of *discipline* on a scientific footing . . .' (Stones and Morris, 1972:14). Using examples of empirical research in various areas, the authors reject 'unscientific and mystical' approaches to teacher education, arguing that teaching problems can be solved by the application of empirical science to the desired objectives.

A crude schematisation of the applied science model of professional education might look like Figure 1.2. It will be seen that, in its extreme form, this model is essentially *one-way*. The findings of scientific knowledge and experimentation are conveyed to the trainee by those who are experts in the relevant areas. Thus, trainee teachers who are concerned with maintaining discipline might receive instruction

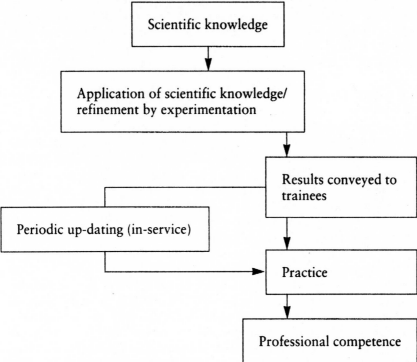

Figure 1.2   Applied science model

from a psychologist on what has been discovered about behaviour modification. It is up to the trainees to put the conclusions from these scientific findings into practice. If the trainees fail, it is perhaps because they haven't understood the findings properly, or because they have not properly applied the findings, or whatever.

It might be, of course, that the problem is not solved because there is something wrong with the scientific knowledge or experimentation base. Indeed, almost by definition, as the professional science develops it brings about changes in the practice element. However, these changes can be established only by those expert in the knowledge or experimental base, and not by the 'practitioners' themselves (i.e. by those actually engaged in the day-to-day practice of the profession). It is possible, of course, for some of the practitioners to become 'experts', but they usually do this by leaving their offices, studios, consulting rooms or classrooms and becoming academics in universities or other institutions of professional education.

This tendency for the experts to be well removed from the day-to-day working scene is more pronounced in teaching than in some other professions. In medicine, for example, a surgeon may have a high academic reputation while at the same time be engaged in the daily performance of surgical operations; General Practitioners, on the other hand, will generally look to other experts for professional updating. Even in such a hard-headed profession as Business Management, there tends to be a fairly clear divide between the 'thinkers' and the 'doers'.

1.9   Separation of research and practice

So we come to another significant way in which teacher education has imitated the development of other professions. This is the almost complete separation between research on the one hand and practice on the other. This separation exists in all major aspects of the two activities. It is true of the people who do the work, the personnel. Researchers and practitioners are usually different people. It is true of the locale, the place where the professional education is done. Usually, professionals acquire their qualifications by leaving, at least temporarily, their place of work. It is also true in terms of the methods of working: the expertise of the trainer is often very different *in kind* from that of the practitioner. Looking at the historical development of what I have here called the applied science model, Schön says (1983:36): 'It was to be the business of the university-based scientists and scholars to create the fundamental theory which professionals and technicians would apply to practice . . . But this division of labour reflected a hierarchy of kinds of knowledge which was also a ladder of status.'

If you think of teacher education, you will probably agree that there is much truth in this. With regard to personnel, professionals who leave the classroom almost never return to it on any long-term basis. With regard to locale, the University Departments of Education and Colleges of Education are physically separated from the schools, apart from the occasional 'demonstration school'. It is true, however, that with the development of agency-based in-service (ABIS), the separation is less complete than it used to be. In ABIS, the trainers operate not within their own base, whether it is a university or college, but within the 'agency' (school, class or department) by which they have been invited to share their expertise. For example, the head of the Modern Languages Department might invite along a university tutor to demonstrate some techniques to develop, say, listening comprehension. This kind of situation tends to put the situation more firmly under the control of the 'clients' (in this case, the modern language teachers), which probably helps to ensure that the tutor's input is guided towards the teachers' needs and interests.

I mentioned earlier the differences between 'experts' and 'practitioners' in terms of expertise. Again, most of us could probably give instances of this from teacher education. Many practising teachers might not be able to understand the more technical research articles, even if they bothered to read them (which few of them do). However, the frustrations, survival techniques and infrequent rewards of teaching in today's classrooms can only be understood by many educational researchers in an abstract way. Indeed, the gulf is sometimes wider than ignorance or status: it can even be one of mutual contempt and antipathy. Researchers can be contemptuous of teachers because 'they never read'. Teachers can be antipathetic to researchers because the latter are seen as 'refugees from the classroom'.

In addition to all this, many practitioners would argue that the applied science approach has failed to 'deliver the goods'. In spite of the vast amount of research that has been done, the most intractable professional problems remain. I mentioned earlier how, in the early 1970s, some experts were making encouraging noises about the study of the problem of discipline being placed on a more scientific footing, allowing the inference to be drawn that empirical research would soon deliver some formula for maintaining discipline. Many of today's teachers will wonder when the expected improvements will take place, and some would argue that the problems of discipline have, in fact, got worse over the last two decades.

More specifically, in the field of language teaching, it could be argued that the most 'scientific' method in recent times was the 'audio-visual' or 'structural drill' method. This methodology was firmly anchored in the 'scientific' basis of the dominant psychological theory of the time, namely Behaviourism.

Many people now claim that this led to unmotivating and irrelevant learning experiences. Yet it is interesting that the 'revolution' which displaced this methodology did not take place at the classroom level (where the damage was allegedly being done), but at the academic level, with the advent of Chomsky's Transformational Generative Grammar (TG). This development, in its turn, led to some bizarre attempts to teach language through 'transformations', which fortunately only lasted a brief time. These attempts took place in spite of the fact that Chomsky himself always questioned whether his findings had any direct application to language teaching. This should warn us to look closely at the 'science' which is being applied. Is it something that has actually been proved, or is it an unjustified analogy imposed on the complexity of teaching? Chomsky showed that many of the Behaviourist 'applications' to language learning were in fact simply analogies, with very little empirical basis.

PERSONAL REVIEW

What areas of 'scientific knowledge' do you think teachers of a foreign language ought to be familiar with? Within those, what broad topics should they be familiar with? Which of these topics are 'desirable' and which are 'essential'?

Is the mastering of such scientific knowledge enough to make a competent teacher? If not, what more is required?

1.10   The reflective model

To some extent, the social respect which professions have depends on the fact that they lay claim to a kind of knowledge that others, who are not members of the profession, are lacking in. What is the nature of this knowledge?

Schön points out that when we refer to 'professional knowledge' we can be talking about one of two different kinds of knowledge. The first kind consists of facts, data and theories, often related to some kind of research. Thus, language teachers might be familiar with certain concepts from the science of linguistics, such as intonation patterns and a grammatical hierarchy from the morpheme to the sentence. They might also be familiar with certain concepts from the science of assessment, such as validity, reliability and so on. This kind of knowledge figures largely in programmes of teacher education for language teachers. Schön does not use a particular term for this kind of knowledge, although he refers to 'research-based theories and techniques' (1983:58). It would be useful to have a specific name for this kind of knowledge, but one is reluctant to specify it all as 'research-based'. I would prefer to call it 'received knowledge', on the grounds that, (a) the trainee has 'received' it rather than 'experienced' it in professional action, and (b) it is a deliberate echo of the phrase 'received wisdom' (meaning what is commonly accepted without proof or question), which it resembles in certain ways.

Many of the ideas and theories which form the input of many education courses are by no means all based on research, however widely defined. For example, some of the rationales for 'Communicative Methodology' which trainee language teachers study today are purely speculative. Sometimes the subjects which a trainee is expected to study are dictated by tradition or convention, rather than by any proven application to the competent practice of the profession. So the phrase 'received knowledge' seems appropriate.

'Received knowledge' is to be contrasted with another type of knowledge which I shall call 'experiential knowledge'. I would define 'experiential knowledge' as deriving from two phenomena described by Schon: 'knowing-in-action' and 'reflection'.

Knowing-in-action Schön describes 'knowing-in-action' this way (1983: 49, 50):

> ' . . . the workaday life of the professional depends upon tacit knowing-in-action. Every competent practitioner can recognise phenomena – families of symptoms associated with a particular disease, peculiarities of a certain building site, irregularities of materials or structures – for which he cannot give a reasonably accurate or complete description. In his day-to-day practice he makes innumerable judgements of quality for which he cannot state adequate criteria, and he displays skills for which he cannot state the rules and procedures. Even when he makes conscious use of research-based theories and techniques, he is dependent on tacit recognitions. Judgements are skilful performances.'

These observations clearly apply to practitioner teachers.

MacLeod and McIntyre (1977:266) comment as follows:

> 'One striking feature of classrooms is the sheer complexity, quantity and rapidity of classroom interaction. As many as 1,000 interpersonal exchanges each day have been observed, and the multiplicity of decisions which have to be made, and the volume of information relevant to each decision are such that for the teacher logical consideration and decision making would seem to be impossible . . .'

What are the cognitive bases of these interactions and decisions, most of which are immediate and many of which are complex? It is clearly not the case that they are based (or even should be based) on a direct application of 'received knowledge'. Some of the issues will not have been dealt with in any definitive way by research. They will certainly not all have been covered by even the most comprehensive training in 'language teaching skills'. Often satisfaction (or unease) is expressed in terms of feeling, rather than a conscious application of principles. The teacher may say of a certain procedure that 'it did not seem to be working well, so I switched to something else'.

Reflection It is possible to leave these feelings or intentions either unexplored or unconsciously stored, or it is possible to reflect on them, leading to the conscious development of insights into knowing-in-action. It is (or should be) normal for professionals to reflect on their professional performance, particularly when it goes especially well or especially badly. They will probably ask themselves what went wrong or why it went so well. They will probably want to think about what to avoid in the future, what to repeat and so on.

It is also possible for this to happen while the process of professional action is actually proceeding. As Schön points out (1983:10), both professionals and lay people, especially when surprised by some unexpected development 'turn thought back on action'. They may ask themselves such questions as 'What features do I notice when I recognize this thing? What are the criteria by which I make this judgement? What procedures am I enacting when I perform this skill? How am I framing the problem that I am trying to solve?' In the answers to these questions, which in a given situation would naturally be expressed in a much less abstract and much more specific way, lies the path to possible self-improvement.

PERSONAL REVIEW

Think back to some incident or development that happened in class which you had not planned for, e.g.
  a disciplinary problem
  an unpredicted error made by a student
  an unexpected lack of understanding
  a decision on your part that you would have to teach the lesson differently from what was planned, etc.

1. What was the problem or development, exactly?
2. How did you handle it?
3. Why did you handle it the way you did?
4. Would you handle it in the same way again? If not, why not?
5. Has the incident changed your general view of how to go about the practice of teaching? (e.g. you may have decided in general to be more strict, to use group work less, to ask more questions, etc.)

1.11 Professional education

Following on from these arguments, it would therefore seem that structured professional education (as in a teacher education course) should include two kinds of knowledge development:

1. **Received knowledge** In this the trainee becomes acquainted with the vocabulary of the subject and the matching concepts, research findings, theories and skills which are widely accepted as being part of the necessary intellectual content of the profession. So, currently, it might be accepted that a skilled language teacher will be able (among many other things) to speak the target language to a reasonable degree of fluency, to organise pair and group work, to

read a simple phonetic transcription, to be familiar with certain grammatical terms and so on.

2. **Experiential knowledge**   Here, the trainee will have developed knowledge-in-action by practice of the profession, and will have had, moreover, the opportunity to reflect on that knowledge-in-action. (It should be noted here that it is also possible to develop experiential knowledge by the *observation* of practice, although this 'knowledge-by-observation' is clearly of a different order from 'knowledge-in-action'.)

We now, therefore, have an alternative model for teacher education, which we shall call the 'reflective model'. This model will be elaborated on in Chapter 4 and subsequently, but its basic elements may be summarised in a preliminary way as in Figure 1.3.

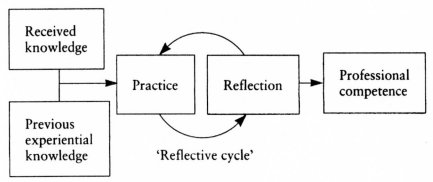

Figure 1.3   Reflective model (preliminary)

1.12   Experiential knowledge and the craft model

It could be said that one of the strengths of the model of teacher education which regarded teaching as a 'craft' was that it gave due recognition to the element of experiential knowledge. It is hopefully now clear why the analogy of teaching as a 'craft' cannot be the whole story. As I have said before, the idea of a 'craft' learned by 'apprentices' is essentially conservative. It implies no change, or very little change over a long period of time. The needs of teaching in a time of very rapid change will obviously not be met by such procedures.

Moreover, the 'craft' training scenario is basically *imitative* in nature. There is certainly a case for the observation of experienced teachers by trainees. In the reflective model, however, such observation will be a matter for reflection rather than imitation, and the reflection will probably have to be carefully structured, so that the trainee can best benefit from the period of observation. Ways in which this might be achieved will be discussed later.

It follows that the traditional use in teacher education of the 'demonstration lesson' is an outmoded strategy, since 'demonstration' usually pre-supposes 'imitation'. The reflective model sees the demonstration lesson as simply another kind of experience to be analysed and reflected on, and then related as appropriate to the trainee's own practice.

It is tempting to say that there are certain aspects of teaching involving brief or superficial techniques which can be and usually are demonstrated in professional learning contexts. With regard to language teaching, one thinks of the tutor demonstrating good use of the blackboard, or showing the trainees how group work can be set up quickly. Yet even here one has to be careful not to claim too much. Mark A. Clarke (1983:109–110) is interesting on this point:

' . . . when one is confronted by a group of intelligent, curious, motivated and totally naive individuals who want to know exactly how to conduct a particular technique, one learns very quickly that nothing can be taken for granted. Perfectly innocent questions suddenly expose the virtually limitless options that are available at each and every step in the execution of technique . . . it soon becomes obvious, in the course of such discussions, that to describe a technique is to trace a line through a complex, shifting series of decision points, and each decision is influenced by an awesome number of variables . . .'

It is clear then that, while some aspects of a professional's work can and should be demonstrated, most are more appropriately the subject of reflection rather than imitation.

1.13 Summary

In this chapter, I have been concerned with establishing the nature of teaching as a professional activity with a view to discovering how such an activity can best be learned. I have discussed three different models of professional preparation. I have called them the 'craft' model, the 'applied science' model, and the 'reflective' model. The 'craft' model gives due value to the experiential aspect of professional development, but is essentially static and imitative. It does not handle satisfactorily the crucial element of the explosive growth of relevant scientific knowledge in recent times.

The 'applied science' model has taken this into account but has led to a split between research and professional practice. This has engendered problems of status which are particularly acute in teaching. There has also been a tendency to downgrade the value of the classroom teacher's expertise derived from experience. Another problem has been the tendency for the 'applied science' model to promise what it has not so far been able to deliver: a 'scientific' solution to very complex professional dilemmas.

I have proposed the 'reflective' model as a compromise solution which gives due weight both to experience and to the scientific basis of the profession. I have suggested, therefore, that teacher education has two main dimensions:

— *'received knowledge'* which includes, among other things, the necessary and valuable element of scientific research, and
— *'experiential knowledge'* which relates to the professional's ongoing experience.

The rest of this book will essentially be an explanation of the implications of this view of teaching and teacher education for the training of language teachers.

PERSONAL REVIEW

In this chapter we have been emphasising the importance of both experiential knowledge and received knowledge.

Look at the following description of a unit on EFL Methodology. Comment on it from the point of view of *process* rather than content (i.e. try not to spend time on criticising the choice of topics!). Firstly, you might like to consider how these sessions could be best organised in terms of experiential learning. What sorts of activities would be most appropriate? What opportunities for experiential learning and reflection could be provided? Would you have the same kind of activity each time or could you vary it?

Secondly, you might want to consider what, if any, elements of 'received knowledge' might be relevant to this unit? How helpful would the teaching of such elements be to the trainees – very helpful or just of marginal help?

Unit: Introduction to Classroom Management (24 hours)

Topics 1. Beginning the lesson
2. Checking attendance
3. Getting organised: seating, books, blackboard
4. Introducing different stages of the lesson
5. Visual aids
6. a) Dividing up the class: choral/individual/teams
   b) Dividing up the class: pair and group work
7. Control and discipline
8. Ending the lesson and setting homework

---

2 Acquiring received knowledge: The learner's perspective

2.1 Overview

In the last chapter, I suggested that professional knowledge is actually made up of two kinds of knowledge, namely 'received knowledge' and 'experiential knowledge'. In this chapter, I will discuss the issue of how received knowledge is to be acquired.

The chapter will begin by making the obvious point that teacher educators should 'practise what they preach'. This will lead on to the discussion of the need for variety in learning modes. I will relate this to the issue of *learning styles*, on which there has been much interesting research. I will, however, suggest that it might be more profitable to think not of learning styles, but of *learning strategies*, and the reasons for this will be discussed. I will then come back to the question of 'practising what you preach' specifically with reference to the reflective model. Finally, the topic of *study skills* in higher education as a method of systematically developing learning strategies will be briefly examined.

2.2 'Practising what you preach'

Trainee teachers and in-service trainees are traditionally critical of the standard of training they receive, and it is natural that this should be the case. In any context where the professional development of teachers is taking place, the nature and quality of the teaching and learning in that context is clearly of crucial importance. Just as in a Medical School clients might be entitled to expect the highest standards of care and hygiene, and in a Business School the highest standards of administrative efficiency, so in a College or Department of Education the clients are entitled to expect the highest standards of teaching.

It is also taken as a truism that the teaching and learning experience in a College or Department of Education ought to reflect, *in an appropriate way*, the teaching and learning experience of the schools that the trainees are going to teach in. The phrase 'in an appropriate way' has been emphasised, because all too often in the past this has meant treating the trainees like schoolchildren! In various parts of the world, there will be cultural norms and expectations for educational institutions at whatever level: this point is not being argued against here, and will obviously be part of the meaning of 'appropriate' in those various educational centres. However, it does seem clear to most people who have written about it that the approach to teaching being put over by the institution ought somehow to be experienced as a reality by the trainees.

Thus, for example, if communicative methodology is the approach to language teaching which the institution has taken on board, then ideally this should be reflected in some, if not all, aspects of the training process. If the trainees are being encouraged to break up large classes into small groups for group interaction, then periodically they ought to find themselves part of a larger class which is being organised in this way. Only by experiencing this as a (sophisticated) consumer can they begin to evaluate it as a valid procedure for their own clients, their students. They are also quite entitled to assume that if this procedure is chaotic and/or unproductive at their level, then it is unlikely to work with students less mature than themselves. If there is an emphasis in the methodology on heuristics (discovery learning), it is unlikely that they will develop much skill or understanding of this technique if they are taught only by didactic lectures and assessed only by examinations which emphasise factual recall.

Let us take one more example: if (as might seem desirable) the trainees are to be encouraged to develop their professional expertise in an autonomous and self-directed way, then somehow autonomy and self-direction should be woven into the fabric of their course. Moreover, one might add, these qualities should also be part of the normal professional experience of their tutors, otherwise how can they meaningfully convey them as desirable qualities to their trainees?

PERSONAL REVIEW

What similarities or differences can you see between the process of, on the one hand, learning a language and, on the other, learning to teach a language? Is there any 'overlap' between the conditions that facilitate both kinds of learning?

For some time now, it has been generally accepted that teachers should motivate their students by introducing variety in their lessons. In recent years, varied modes of learning have also become common in professional education including, of course, teacher education. This development is, one hopes, another aspect of 'practising what you preach'. However, there are other reasons why this introduction of varied learning modes is a desirable development. Some of these have been the subject of interesting research studies, and I will give a few examples of these in the following section.

2.3 Styles of learning

Someone once said: 'In one sense, all students are different; in another sense, all students are the same.' Tutors and teachers will no doubt read their own meanings into this rather enigmatic remark, but most tutors would probably agree, from their own experience and observation, that different students certainly learn in different ways. In recent years, some very interesting research has been devoted to refining this insight. For a lucid and fascinating account of this work, read Noel Entwistle's *Styles of Learning and Teaching* (1981).

Hudson (1968) and Parlett (1970), for example, divide students into those who are *syllabus-bound* and those who are *syllabus-free*. Main (1980:10) summarises the difference thus: 'Syllabus-bound students need exams in order to study, do not read widely outside the set work, attend classes regularly and may very well have conscientious study habits'; the syllabus-free students, on the other hand, 'operate better when they can pursue their own lines of work, and often feel restricted by course requirements'.

A different kind of distinction is made by Miller and Parlett (1974), who have three categories of students: the *cue-seekers*, who actively elicit from their tutors information about their course, examinations, etc.; the *cue-conscious*, who are able to pick up useful hints that are passed on by tutors concerning the organisation of their courses or whatever; and the *cue-deaf*, who do not respond to such hints or information. Fortunately, there is a tendency in recent years for course descriptions to be much more explicit in stating exactly what is to be expected of students, and how they will be graded, etc. Criteria for assignments and examinations, for example, tend to be made explicit and public more often. Clearing away the fog of mystery surrounding course objectives, assessment, and so on can only be a good thing, and should make the kind of expertise that Miller and Parlett refer to less critical. Presumably, however, it will never disappear entirely: the student who is alert to finding out the 'rules of the game' will always be at an advantage.

A very different, and in some ways more central, aspect of the study process has been researched by Ference Marton and others at Gothenburg and by Noel Entwistle and others at Lancaster (described in Entwistle, 1981: 75ff).

This research related to discovering how students tackled the task of reading academic articles or texts. Each student was asked in her own time (all the students were female) to read a 1,500 word article on which she was subsequently interviewed. When these interviews were transcribed and analysed, they revealed a clear-cut distinction between the students, related to the *depth of understanding* that the students pursued:

1. **Deep processing approach**   In this approach the students were concerned with the overall meaning of the article, and with understanding the author's basic arguments. The main emphasis was therefore on *understanding*.
2. **Surface processing approach**   The students who adopted this approach were much more concerned with the surface representation of the article, for example, by attempting to memorise details, or even the actual words used in the passage. The main emphasis was therefore on *rote-learning*.

Cutting across these two categories were two other categories which related to the students' *personal involvement* with the text, characterised as *active* and *passive*. Students who were actively involved with the passage put a lot of themselves into the task. A Lancaster student using the *deep active* approach, for example, tried to relate her understanding of the author's main points to her own personal experience; another student, using the *surface active* approach concentrated hard on the article by trying to memorise names and data from it.

A student reading the article in a *deep passive* manner, on the other hand, went for the main ideas but in a 'casual' and 'impartial' way, with very little personal involvement. The *surface passive* approach of another student was characterised by a hurried, uninterested surface reading, paying very little attention to the gist of the author's message.

Further research was done to discover the effectiveness of these learning styles, both in terms of understanding of the input text, and in terms of subsequent examination performance.

Perhaps predictably, the deep approach to study of the article proved to be much more effective (100% of the deep processors showing a 'high' level of understanding, and 93% of the surface processors showing a 'low' level of understanding). In examinations, 90% of those who consistently employed a deep approach in both the experiment and normal studies passed all their examinations, whereas only 23% of those employing a consistently surface approach passed all theirs.

Another profound distinction is made by Pask and Scott (1972), who divide students who are required to reach a deep level of understanding into *serialists* and *holists*. Serialists like to proceed step by step, mastering one thing at a time; holists like to get an overview, to make global hypotheses which are checked against experience, and restructured if necessary. Both of these strategies can lead to deep understanding but each of them carries its own dangers if handled badly: the holist, for example, may be over-ready to form hasty, personal judgements, while the serialist may not be finally aware of how the various elements of the topic relate to one another.

PERSONAL REVIEW

1. Select any moderately difficult article on language teaching or applied linguistics, etc. that you have not read before. Read it to get the gist or general meaning of the article. Read it as many times as you like and in whatever way you prefer until you are satisfied that you have got the main ideas. Make a short list of the main ideas.

2. How did you go about studying the passage? Were there any particular techniques you used, e.g. reading some sentences again, reading the whole text, or part of it, more than once, etc. Compare your approach to this task with others. Did you all do it the same way?

3. Can you think of any other ways you could have read the article? If you think of some, are you tempted to experiment with them, or do you think you will stick to the method you used in this case?

The various learning styles that have been discussed here are listed in Figure 2.1. An attempt has been made to display them in a way which points up some areas of similarity or significant overlap among the different styles. It should, however, be borne in mind that the relationship between these styles is not at all simple or straightforward.

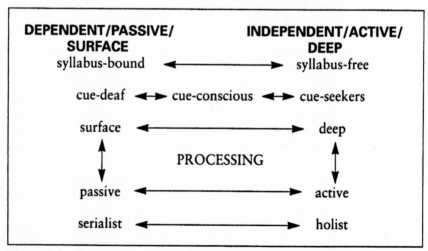

Figure 2.1   Some parameters of learning styles

PERSONAL REVIEW

Think about the different styles of learning that have been
discussed in this section. Which of them apply to you, do you
think? Are there any other differences in learning, in your
experience, that have not been noted in this section?

2.4 How crucial are learning styles?

It will be clear from the previous sections that the issue of learning styles
has raised a tremendous amount of interest among academics. This has
resulted in much interesting research which has thrown light on the
various ways in which students react individually to the learning
process. In this section, I will try to put this work in perspective, by
asking two questions: (1) How do learning styles relate to other factors
affecting individual students? and (2) Are students 'prisoners' (as it
were) of their learning styles?

In responding to the first question, one may note that, while learning
styles are undoubtedly important, they are only one aspect of a whole
range of individual differences in students. For example, Entwistle
(1981:247) lists the following 'student characteristics':

> previous knowledge
> intellectual skills
> types and levels of motivation
> interests
> level of anxiety
> preferred learning style
> expectations about what is to be learned

It is also worth noting that, as with most types of psychological
distinction, comparatively few people may be absolutely clear and
typical examples of a given category, with most people falling within a
grey category which is somewhere in the middle. For example, in the
research by Marton referred to in the previous section, not all the
students used a deep or surface approach consistently, and indeed, in the
original experiment, 30% of the students involved could not be confi-
dently assigned to either category.

This brings us on to the second question posed at the beginning of this
section: Are students the prisoners of their learning styles? Pask notes
that many students can and should use both serialist and holist strategies
– using, in fact, a *versatile* learning style. There is also evidence that

B

students in higher education often abandon less effective learning styles and develop more effective styles. Indeed, it could be argued that higher education has failed them if they do not do so!

Some interesting research done in the United States refers precisely to this process of intellectual development. The research was done by Roy Heath at Princeton University (Heath, 1964, 1978, summarised in Entwistle, 1981:67–71), and relates to a group of 36 male students, to whom he was an academic counsellor from the mid 1950s until the time of their graduation. He found that, initially, his students could be divided into three types. First, there were the 'non-committers', who avoided involvement as far as possible, thus providing themselves with a foolproof excuse for lack of success – if they *had* bothered to involve themselves, they would have been successful! Secondly, there were the 'hustlers', who were very competitive types: university life was a kind of battle, and you had to be ruthless to win. Thirdly, there were the 'plungers', who suffered from extremes of mood, and corresponding differences in motivation and achievement. The important thing to note is that all these students changed and matured during their time at Princeton, eventually approximating (to a greater or lesser degree) to a fourth type, which Heath calls the 'reasonable adventurer'. When 'reasonable adventurers' are confronted with a problem they alternate between two stages: one stage is intellectual involvement and excitement (the 'adventurer' stage) and the other a stage in which they stand back from the evidence and coolly evaluate it (the 'reasonable' stage).

It is worth noting that the students' *personalities* did not change: they were still 'hustlers' or 'plungers', etc. by nature, but their intellectual approach matured, so that the vast majority of those who graduated with honours were of the 'reasonable adventurer' type – and presumably Princeton could take some of the credit for fostering this process of intellectual maturation.

PERSONAL REVIEW

Do you think you go about studying now in the same way as you did when you were at secondary school? If you have changed, what is the nature of the change? Have you acquired any new learning techniques? Has your *attitude* to learning changed?

If your way of learning has not changed, is this because you have not seen a need to change, or for some other reason (e.g. not being aware of the techniques)?

What is your attitude towards Heath's research into the way that his university students changed over time? Do you think such change is inevitable and/or desirable?

Perhaps I should strike a note of caution at this point. You will perhaps have noted that most of the research referred to here has been done in American and European universities and colleges. It may be that some of the attitudes to learning that have been discussed are influenced as much by cultural as by personal factors. They should, therefore, not be applied uncritically to other cultural contexts. Tutors from such contexts should check these findings against their own experience, before applying them. (It would also, of course, be very interesting if they could verify them experimentally for their own groups of students.)

2.5 Learning strategies

In the previous section, I reviewed some evidence that students need not be, or need not remain, restricted and confused by the learning style that comes naturally to them. It might be, therefore, that teacher educators should focus on the concept of *learning strategies* rather than learning styles.

There would be various consequences of such an approach. First of all, trainees should be aware that there is a variety of ways of learning. Some of these learning modes will come naturally to certain trainees. Other learning modes may have to be experimented with, and some of these may also be found useful. In other words, trainees should be made a little bit more self-conscious about the actual *process* of study. (I will come back to this when dealing with study skills in section 2.7.)

Secondly, trainees should be exposed to a variety of learning contexts in which they can explore and develop their learning strategies. It is perhaps doing trainees a disservice to lock them into one particular mode of learning, even if that mode of learning is congenial to them.

Thirdly, trainees should be encouraged to think strategically about their learning. They should ask themselves questions like: What sort of learning is required here? What is the most effective and time-saving method of doing that learning? (There are, for example, efficient ways of managing rote-learning and other ways which are much less efficient.)

2.6 Learning strategies in teacher education

We have seen why it is desirable that educational institutions should expose trainees to a *variety* of learning experiences. This would ensure that no particular learning style was unduly neglected, and would also hopefully extend the trainees' repertoire of learning strategies.

Still following on from what I said earlier about 'practising what you preach', it might also be argued that the institution ought to go further and attempt to foster those learning strategies which best fit in with the espoused model of professional development. Thus, if it were thought desirable, as was argued in the previous chapter, that teachers ought to be encouraged to become 'reflective practitioners', developing by reflecting on their professional experience, then it follows that a good part of their learning in the college or university ought to be experiential in nature.

Similarly, it may be the case that the teachers in the field are seen as not simply (at best) followers of instructions, but professionals who are open to new ideas, while being at the same time, practical and sensible in selecting and applying them. It seems desirable that such teachers should be flexible, capable of further independent study, able to solve problems in a rational way, able to combine speed of response with depth of understanding, and so on. This more ambitious aim would clearly demand a correspondingly high quality of trainee teacher, approximating more to Heath's 'reasonable adventurer'. And, finally, one might argue that any effective programme of teacher education ought to involve a fair amount of 'deep processing' of inputs.

These aims do not seem outlandish or impossible, although not all the trainees might attain them, nor would they necessarily be required to attain them, depending on the public expectations about their subsequent level of professional action.

In the next chapter, I shall discuss the *teaching* strategies which might facilitate the acquisition of the learning strategies appropriate to teacher education. Before leaving this topic, however, it is important to address the question of whether or not trainees can be taught how to study, and, if so, what is the best method of organising this.

2.7 Study skills

This is a large subject, and I am not going to attempt, in these few pages, to deal with it in any detailed way: broad principles and approaches only will be discussed.

It must be admitted immediately that it is artificial and to some extent misleading to discuss the acquisition of study skills apart from other aspects of a course in higher education. Clearly, no amount of training in 'note taking' can compensate for lectures that are disorganised, irrelevant and boring; no amount of training in 'reading skills' can make up for reading lists that are unrealistically long and only sporadically relevant, and so on. Good learning techniques and good teaching and assessment techniques are two sides of the same coin. Both sets of techniques should have equal priority, and it is to be regretted that, usually for the wrong kind of 'professional' reasons, this is seldom the case (except, of course, in institutions where neither of them has any priority at all).

The whole issue of whether and how study skills ought to be taught is hotly debated and has given rise to widely divergent views (for a brief but balanced and authoritative survey of the issue, see Beard and Hartley, 1984: 119–127).

Beard and Hartley conclude (p.127) that students need to develop effective study skills if they are to become effective independent learners. There is evidence that training in library skills is valuable, and that speed-reading courses may improve reading speeds but that only some students sustain the improvement. Note taking can aid learning and recall in certain situations. There is, therefore, some substantive empirical evidence for the view which most people take (including many students, judging from the number of self-help study-skills books on the market) that time spent on developing study skills is worthwhile.

How are study skills to be taught? If it is the aim of the teacher education course to develop 'reflective practitioners' then there might be a good case for getting the trainees to reflect on what I have elsewhere called *study process* (Wallace, 1982). The basic idea of this approach relates to an understanding, on the part of the trainees, on why their learning is organised the way it is (whatever that way might be). They may be asked to consider such questions as: Why do we sometimes learn from books and sometimes from lectures? What is the value of discussing something as opposed to, say, listening to the lecturer's conclusions in the form of a lecture? What constitutes effective participation in a discussion and what does not? What is the difference (if any) between essays and examination answers? It would clearly be helpful for tutors and trainees to explore these questions together.

The next stage might well be for trainees to go on to reflect on their own study habits by undertaking learning tasks and comparing their own strategies, techniques or procedures with their fellow trainees. This is, indeed, a procedure which we have already used in this chapter (e.g. the 'Personal review' on page 22). Graham Gibbs in his book *Teaching Students to Learn* (1981) has some excellent suggestions about how this 'student-centred' approach might work, with very practical exercises which can be used as they are, or adapted to local circumstances.

Once the trainees' awareness of their needs has been raised, this can be followed up with sessions on helpful techniques and suggestions related to their perceived needs and the tutors' expectations. There are, fortunately, an increasing number of resources available to help the tutor with teaching material, although some of them may have to be adapted to suit local needs. Best of all, of course, would be material generated by the tutors themselves.

Summary

We have seen how different people have different attitudes to learning and their own individual ways of learning. Where these are unconscious, or an integral part of the learner's personality, we have called them *learning styles*. However, there is evidence that people can also have considerable control over which style of learning they use in particular situations, so it might be more appropriate to focus on the idea of *learning strategies*, which trainees can adopt as required. These differences imply the need for a corresponding variety of teaching strategies.

There is also evidence that people benefit from study-skill programmes to improve their learning. The most appropriate way forward might be for the trainees to be encouraged to reflect on the different methods of learning available to them ('study process'), and also to reflect on their own learning strategies in a variety of learning tasks. On this reflective basis, they can be introduced to other strategies and specific techniques which will extend their learning repertoire.

PERSONAL REVIEW

Using your own experience as a learner, think of those factors which are the *teacher's responsibility*, or to some extent *under the teacher's control*, (e.g. classroom situations, teaching methods, teacher attitudes, etc.), and which help you to learn, or make it easy for you to learn. Also, think of the factors that make it difficult for you to learn. Compare your experience with others. What conclusions do you draw? Can you relate your conclusions to what you have learned in this chapter?

---

3 Modes of teaching and learning in teacher education courses

3.1 Overview

Following on from the previous chapter, I will argue that a variety of ways or methods ('modes') of teaching and learning should be used in teacher education courses. These various teaching and learning modes should be clearly and consciously related to various teaching and learning purposes. The methodology and strengths and weaknesses of certain common teaching and learning modes (concentrating on the lecture and discussion modes) will be reviewed briefly. If any of the terms used in this chapter to describe certain teaching modes are new to you, please note that there is a glossary at the end of the chapter, on page 44.

3.2 Variety of learning experiences

One of the most striking features of many higher education programmes is the very restricted range of teaching and learning modes that are utilised. In some institutions, the dominant teaching mode is the formal lecture, perhaps backed up by tutorials; at the other extreme, it might be the individual tutorial, perhaps with optional lectures. What is even more disappointing is the reason for certain modes being dominant: often it is a matter of unthinking tradition ('this is the way it has always been done'), sometimes linked to administrative convenience ('it's easy to organise').

There are several reasons which could be presented for involving trainees in a variety of teaching and learning modes:

1. As we have seen, trainees' learning styles vary, and this should be reflected in teaching strategies.
2. It has also been previously argued that trainees ought to be encouraged to experiment with a variety of learning strategies.
3. To avoid boredom: as in most other aspects of life, variety adds spice and stimulus to the learning process.
4. Variety makes teaching more interesting for the tutor also: too

much predictability in teaching situations leads to mechanical teaching.

5. The tutor gets to know her trainees better and is better able to evaluate them fairly by seeing them operate in a variety of learning situations.
6. Different learning experiences are more appropriate to different learning purposes. (This point will be discussed in greater depth later.)

Finally, trainee teachers are often criticised for not providing enough variety of activities in their lessons. It seems sensible, therefore, that variety of presentation should be demonstrated (as far as is appropriate) in the situations where the trainees themselves are being taught.

PERSONAL REVIEW

It is always an interesting exercise to get a group of teachers together and to ask them to list as many teaching and learning activities suitable for higher education they can think of. The group is almost always astonished at the huge variety of activities that ultimately results from this kind of 'brainstorming' process. You might care to try this for yourself and see how many you can get. When you have done this, you might find it useful to check your list against the glossary of teaching and learning modes in higher education which is at the end of this chapter, on page 44.

3.3 Categorising teaching and learning modes

Hopefully, your 'Personal review' in the previous section will have shown you that there is a great variety of possible teaching and learning modes. With such richness of possibilities, it might be useful to think of ways of broadly categorising these activities. Here again there are all kinds of possibilities according to the aspect we wish to focus on. Here are some suggestions:

1. **How much tutor–trainee interaction?** This is probably the category which would occur immediately to most people, with the formal lecture (or in distance learning, the televised lecture) near one end of the scale, and a lively discussion group near the other.
2. **How much tutor control?** Here again, at one extreme we would have the formal lecture and the tutorless group at the other.
3. **How much attention to the individual?** Here one might contrast, say, a class essay with a computer assisted learning programme.

4. **How applicational?** One might contrast reading a theoretical textbook with working on a case study.
5. **How much scope for expression of feelings?** Feelings are always present in human interaction and it is foolish to ignore them or pretend they don't exist (see Bramley, 1979). Some activities inhibit the expression of fears, anxieties and other feelings, whereas others (e.g. counselling sessions) should allow personal feelings to surface.
6. **How is the class physically organised?** Certain furniture arrangements encourage one kind of activity or interaction and tend to discourage another.
7. **What is the source of teaching support and how is it used?** Teaching sessions may utilise one or more kinds of teaching support (e.g. blackboard, audio, video, etc.), and they may differ as to how far any particular support is exploited. For example, a tutor may design her whole session round a video input, with pre-viewing tasks, tasks while viewing (filling in checklists, etc.) and post-viewing discussion; or the input may be used briefly to illustrate a point.

The importance of each, or all, of the categories above depends on another question: what is the purpose of any given teaching session? It is to this issue that we turn in the next section.

PERSONAL REVIEW

Select what, to your mind, are the most important or commonly used modes that you are familiar with. Look at the categories listed above. Apply these categories to each of the modes in turn. Can you draw any conclusions from your categorisation of these modes? Do the modes complement one another or are they all doing more or less the same kind of thing?

3.4 Modes and purposes

Relating modes and purposes

It will be immediately clear that there is no one-to-one relationship between modes and purposes; in other words, it is not usually the case that any given mode may fulfil only one purpose or that any given purpose may only be met by using one mode. If we take the lecture mode, as a case in point, it is clear that it may be used to meet a wide variety of purposes. A lecture may be used, for example, to provide guidelines for a subject that is new to the trainees. It may be intended to stimulate the trainees by posing an interesting problem, or by showing the relevance of the topic to the trainees' professional concerns. The lecture may be intended to demonstrate the methodology of the subject: to show how a problem would be solved within the given subject area using the techniques appropriate to that subject.

Once the purpose is clarified it may be discovered, of course, that it might be best met by using a totally different mode, or by using some different approach within the given mode. For example, the tutor's purpose may be 'to stimulate thought' about a particular topic, but there is evidence which suggests that lectures are less effective for this purpose than small group discussions and projects (Bligh, 1971). Alternatively, the tutor might decide to integrate some kind of discussion or feedback session into her lecture.

If, on the other hand, we start with a purpose, for example, conveying information, this may be done effectively in a whole variety of ways: by a handout, by lecture, by reference to a chapter in a standard textbook, and so on.

Teaching and learning purposes

There are two ways for a tutor to consider the purpose of a teaching session. The first, and notably the one which comes most naturally, is for the tutor to think in terms of her own behaviour, what she is going to do, for example, to provide an overview of a subject, or to list a number of facts. Here is a list of possible teaching purposes:

1. Provide an *overview* of a subject.
2. *List* a number of reasons, facts, etc.
3. *Report* on research, etc.
4. *Summarise* findings, etc.
5. *Contrast* two or more approaches, etc.
6. *Argue* a case.
7. *Illustrate* a technique.
8. *Apply* theories, findings.
9. *Analyse* a complex situation.
10. *Synthesise* different approaches.
11. *Evaluate* evidence.
12. *Stimulate* thoughts and feelings. *Generate* ideas.

Looking at it from another angle, however, we might comment that presumably these activities are intended to involve the trainees in some kind of learning. For example, if we take purpose 11 above (evaluate evidence), is the intention simply to provide the trainees with a considered and authoritative judgement on the issue, or is it intended to demonstrate to them how evidence should be evaluated? Or is it a combination of both? Sometimes, it is quite easy for the tutor to assess whether her own teaching purpose has been achieved – especially if it is simply a matter of providing factual information through a lecture. But if the intention is the more ambitious one of, for example, showing the trainees how to evaluate evidence, then the assessment of success is more problematic. What opportunity has been given to the trainees to evaluate the evidence for themselves? What indication is there of their success or failure? Getting this kind of feedback may require more careful planning and perhaps more varied techniques.

PERSONAL REVIEW

You are now invited to put yourself in the trainees' shoes, as it were, and to think of learning purposes. Perhaps the most obvious learning purpose which springs immediately to mind is the acquisition of new knowledge. Starting with that one, try to make a list of *learning* purposes similar to the list of *teaching* purposes on page 32, underlining the key words or phrases.

It should now be clear that in higher education, as in every other kind of education, it is important to think in terms of learning outcomes. The question is not just 'What do I, as a tutor, intend to do?' but also 'What outcome do I expect for the trainees?'

PERSONAL REVIEW

Pick a mode of learning or teaching that you habitually use. Make a list of the possible teaching or learning purposes. Do you use the same mode for all these purposes, or just some of them? What learning outcomes do you expect? How can you evaluate whether those outcomes have actually been achieved?

3.5 Key aspects of the academic process

Following on from, and adapting, work done by Parker and Rubin (1966, discussed in Jaques, 1984:80–1), we might posit that the following four possible key aspects of the academic process would apply to many topic areas:

1. **Acquisition**   Knowledge can be acquired from books, lectures, handouts, etc. It can also be created by discussion, brainstorming, elicitation by question and answer, and so on.
2. **Reflection**   There are two aspects in the handling of new knowledge:
    i) *Deep processing*, in which the trainee develops an understanding of the essential underlying meaning of the new knowledge.
    ii) *Active processing*, in which the trainee relates the new knowledge to her previous knowledge and experience.
3. **Application**   Here the trainee applies new knowledge to the solution of practical problems.
4. **Evaluation**   There are also two aspects to the evaluation stage:
    i) *Trainee evaluation of content and process*, in which the trainee evaluates the new information which she has received and how it has been presented. How valid is it? How useful is its application? Is there anything more that should be known about it? Was it easy to follow? Was its relevance made clear? Could it have been presented in a different way?
    ii) *Assessment*   The assessment procedures should reveal to the trainees and the tutor how far the course objectives have been achieved by each individual trainee.

In the next sections, we shall examine two of the common teaching modes in greater detail.

3.6   Lecture mode

Like all the other modes, the lecture mode has certain advantages and disadvantages. The secret of success in using it is to maximise the advantages and minimise the disadvantages.

Some of the main advantages of the lecture mode are administrative: it is cheap in terms of human resources (the lecturer may address hundreds of people) and it is relatively simple to arrange, if the accommodation is available. Whether lecturing is also cheap in terms of the learning achieved by the trainees is, of course, another matter. Effectively delivering a good lecture to a large audience demands high presentational skills.

It is also a flexible technique. Most or all of the 'teaching' purposes listed in section 3.5 above can be achieved by a well-presented lecture. (As I keep insisting, achievement of learning outcomes is another matter.)

The lecture mode provides human contact in a way that reading, for example, does not. The heightened, almost theatrical, atmosphere of a crowded lecture hall can provide a tutor with a chance to influence her audience in ways that might not be possible even in a discussion group.

There are also certain disadvantages. The most serious, even for a good lecturer, is probably that of sustaining the listener's attention. Fifty or sixty minutes is a long time to spend listening: there is research to show that there is almost universally a drop in attention after fifteen or twenty minutes. (See Bligh, 1971, who uses the term 'microsleeps'!)

The second major disadvantage is the lack of feedback. The larger the audience the more likelihood that they will have come with different expectations, different previous knowledge and even different levels of ability. Very often lecturers can only guess at what effect, if any, their presentation is having on their audience.

The lecturer should therefore maximise the human contact aspect. Eye contact is important. The voice must be projected. A certain amount of gesture (e.g. for emphasis) may be helpful. Within reason, a certain amount of personal anecdote may be appropriate. It may be useful to set aside certain times in the lecture when the audience might be asked to devote all their attention to the lecturer, i.e. not taking notes, which may be taken at other times. Above all, there must be obvious personal commitment on the part of the lecturer. What is it you want to impress on your audience? Even if you wish simply to leave your audience thoughtful and questioning, they must be persuaded that they have something important and worthwhile to be thoughtful or questioning about.

The problem of the attention span may be overcome in various ways. Liveliness of presentation is obviously important. The lecturer may vary the pace, as has been suggested, for example, by getting the trainees sometimes to listen only and at other times to take notes. The use of audio-visual aids can introduce variety and change.

One of the most useful techniques, which can also be used to overcome the problem of lack of feedback, is to introduce some interactive activities (which in the theatre would be called 'audience participation'). A technique commonly used now is that of the 'buzz group'.

After, say twenty minutes, or whenever the lecturer thinks her audience's attention may be beginning to flag, she can set them some easily explained and specific task, for example, 'You have five minutes to see if you can think of three arguments against the view that I have just been explaining to you. You can discuss it in groups of four or five with the people nearest to you.' After five minutes, a few people can be asked to give their views, and their answers can be used as a link on to the next section of the lecture.

Alternatively, the lecture can be stopped after about forty minutes and a list of, say, five short questions may be given to the audience to check their understanding (quiz technique). As a variation on this, the audience may be given the questions at the beginning, and alerted to the fact that they will be asked to answer these questions at the end. The lecturer may check a few of the answer sheets to get some kind of feedback, however partial, and, of course, finally the questions would be checked and answered orally.

Various findings among university students (e.g. Marris, 1964) show that one of the most valued qualities of a lecture in the view of many students is clarity of presentation. There are various ways to achieve this valued quality:

1. **Linkage**   By this I mean consciously relating what you are going to say either to previous lectures or to some area of knowledge or experience that is familiar to your audience. The distinguished American psychologist Ausubel has persuasively argued that no learning can take place which is not anchored in previous learning, and there are benefits to be gained from making explicit links to the previous material (see, for example, Ausubel, 1965).

2. **Briefing**   This is a term used by Gibbs, Habeshaw and Habeshaw (1987) to refer to a procedure by which the speaker makes it clear what purpose she has in mind, and what kind of learning activity she expects the audience to undertake, for example, whether they are expected to take detailed notes, or whether they should only listen carefully because a handout will be given at the end. If she were going to use a buzz group or a quiz, this could also be indicated during the briefing.

3. **Overview**   The purpose of this is to indicate the gist and outline structure of the presentation. It can be extremely helpful to the audience if the lecturer indicates, for example, that she is going to put forward four main arguments and that she is going to use one or two examples to support each argument. (Of course, this information can also be provided by handout, OHP or blackboard outline.)

4. **Signposting**   The purpose of this is to indicate clearly what point in the presentation the lecturer is currently at. To do this, she will use expressions like 'My first point is . . .', 'One final example . . .', 'Finally, to summarise what I've said . . .', etc. These signals are extremely important for clear and helpful notes.

5. **Final summary**   This is invaluable to the audience as a check on their notes, so that they can ensure that they have got the gist or main points of the speaker's message.

PERSONAL REVIEW

If you normally give lectures, use an audio tape to tape the first twenty minutes of a typical lecture. Do you use Linkage, Briefing, Overview and Signposting? If you do, how were they used? If not, do you think any of them could have been used in your lecture? What difference would it have made, do you think?

Consideration of these guidelines should not be taken to indicate that lecturing should be reduced to a formula. There is always the need for variety, so sometimes lectures could be introduced by an anecdote, sometimes by posing a problem, sometimes by contrasting two views, sometimes by a quotation from a famous writer, sometimes by stating an unconventional or extreme point of view, etc. Similarly, changes can be rung on the ways in which lectures are organised and developed, the kinds of interactive activities used, the kinds of learning support utilised and so on, provided the audience is adequately briefed on what to expect. A balance has to be struck between overpredictable routine on the one hand and creating confusion or uncertainty in the trainees' minds on the other.

3.7 Group mode

The group mode is distinguished from the lecture mode in that, while the latter is essentially a one-way process (lecturer – trainees), the former is essentially interactive in nature. The distinction in practice is by no means so clear-cut, as we have already seen. Lectures can be interrupted by other activities, and informal lectures may involve a fair amount of interaction. Nevertheless, the essential distinction is clear. Let us now look at some of the strengths of the group mode.

Group mode: Variety

One of the main advantages of the group mode is the rich variety of different kinds of activity it potentially encompasses. Perhaps this rich complexity may be simplified somewhat if we think in terms of four common types of group organisation, as follows:

1. **Seminars and tutorials**   In these sessions, the main focus is usually on discussion, which may be structured in various ways, for example, by papers presented by one or more participants (a seminar) or arising from topics suggested by the tutor, arising from a previous lecture, or as a result of an essay written by a trainee, and so on. These meetings can be quite formally organised (as seminars usually are) or they can be almost completely unstructured and free-wheeling.

2. **Cross-group activities**   In these sessions, a class is divided into smaller groups, which then interact in various ways. We have already mentioned how a large lecture audience can be divided into 'buzz' groups which then share their findings (or some of them) with the larger group. Another possibility along these lines is the formation of 'pyramid' or 'snowball' groups, in which an individual or small group (let us say a group of two) draws up a list of suggestions or ideas, or whatever. These are then shared with another of the sub-groups (making a group of four), and some of the ideas are agreed on, and others rejected. The groups are doubled again, sharing their ideas and making choices. This process goes on until at some stage there is a plenary session in which the whole class discusses the ideas and suggestions which finally emerge from this filtering process. This technique allows everyone to have a say, without at the end producing an unwieldy collection of views, suggestions or whatever.

    In 'cross-over' groups, the class is divided into groups which discuss the target issues. At the end of a specified period, one or more members of each group 'crosses over' and joins one of the other groups, sharing the views, etc. of her own group with the new group. This has the desirable effect that each group has to agree on what it has decided before it can dispatch its representative(s) to the next group so that its views can be explained to the members of that other group.

3. **Workshops and practical sessions**   Here, the emphasis is on the completion of a practical task which has a highly specific observable outcome. A common workshop activity in a teacher education methodology course is the preparation of teaching materials, but there are clearly many practical activities and exercises across a range of topics which fall into this category.

    One of the principal justifications for workshops and practical sessions in the context of educational learning theory is in terms of what Bruner has called 'the heuristics of discovery' (Bruner, 1965:618). His theory is that it is just as important (perhaps more important) to learn how to solve problems in general, as to learn the solution to any one particular problem. A useful skill for tutors to master when organising workshops and practical sessions is, therefore, the art of making issues 'problematic', i.e. turning teaching points round so that they become problems or puzzles to be solved by trainees using their own ingenuity, background knowledge, work experience or whatever. Let us imagine, for example, that a linguistics tutor who is concerned with the topic of discourse organisation wishes to broach the topic of cohesion (how sentences relate to one another to form a text).

There are at least two ways in which this topic could be tackled. One would be to take a list of categories for types of cohesion from a standard work on the subject, such as in Halliday and Hasan (1976). The trainees could then apply these categories to the analysis of a given text. This would be an expository approach with practical follow-up. On the other hand, the tutor could start with the text and invite the trainees to discover for themselves, in group workshops, what features made the text something more than a jumble of sentences. Subsequent to this, the findings of the different groups could be pooled, and the categories that emerged contrasted with the list that the tutor had previously prepared using authoritative sources. This would be an essentially heuristic approach. (For a thorough working out of this approach, see Adrian Doff's excellent book *Teach English: A training course for teachers*.) Each approach has its own strengths, and also possible dangers.

PERSONAL REVIEW

In the example above, which of the two approaches would you prefer to use, and why?
Take any topic in your area of expertise that you would normally deal with in an expository way, i.e. by simply 'telling' or 'explaining'. Think how you could make it 'problematic' by turning it into a heuristic exercise or workshop. What benefits (if any!) may result from the heuristic approach in this particular case? What dangers might you have to guard against?

---

4. **Simulations, case studies and games**   These sessions are often similar in nature to those in the previous category. The general approach here is somewhat paradoxical in that it attempts to make the classroom activity more relevant and 'real' by introducing an element of 'make-believe'.

Simulations   In 'simulations' the trainees may take the part of certain roles, for example, the roles of 'Director of Studies' and 'Student', 'Head of Department' and 'Assistant Teacher', 'Teacher' and 'Student', and so on. (It is perhaps worth noting that although *role play* is common in this kind of situation, it is not always necessary. In some in-service training simulations, participants may be enacting their real-life roles.) A scenario is also usually provided (e.g. a student complaint, discussion of a new syllabus, presenting a new teaching item, etc.). The trainees act out their roles in the situation, and then discuss their findings.

Case studies   In a 'case study' the data for discussion and analysis is taken from an actual 'case'. Thus, a case study designed to explore the difficulties of implementing a new language syllabus may be based on the experience of a country where such a syllabus has been introduced. The trainee will be provided with, for example, policy documents from the Ministry of Education, a copy of the old syllabus, a copy of the new syllabus, examples of the teaching materials (new and old), evaluation and research reports, and so on. Doing a case study properly obviously involves a tremendous amount of work and time, but nevertheless it is highly valued in management studies, for example, where it is seen as a way of bringing together a whole range of theoretical issues and applying them to a 'real-life' context.

Games   'Games' are usually much more sophisticated in training terms than the language learning games that most language teachers are familiar with. Nevertheless, the general approach and intention are somewhat similar. A simple example is 'The Academic Achievement Game' devised by Entwistle and Wilson (1977). It is a board game played with dice, in which the first person who reaches the 'graduation square' wins. The game has the serious function of raising the awareness of trainees about certain research findings relating to academic achievement.

These three categories obviously interact and overlap in various ways, for example, games can take the form of simulations, case studies can culminate in role playing simulations, and so on.

Group mode: Feedback

If variety and flexibility are a major advantage of the group mode, a further major advantage is in terms of the feedback it provides. This feedback may take many different forms. There is feedback to the tutor in terms of how far the material under discussion is pitched at the right level. Is it obviously flummoxing the participants, or is it perhaps insufficiently challenging for the majority of them? There is feedback to the trainees themselves: they will find it much easier in a less formal setting to get information from the tutor and also to clarify unclear issues with one another. There may also be feedback on the different levels of ability and the different attitudes of the various members of the group which may be invaluable for the successful conduct of the course.

Group mode: Reflection

It will be clear from many of the activities described above that the group mode can provide ample scope for reflection, particularly in terms of trainees being able to relate new information and ideas to their own previous knowledge and professional concerns. Discussion allows them to articulate their own perception of the new ideas, and practical sessions allow them to apply theoretical knowledge to realistic or quasi-realistic situations and to monitor the outcome.

Group mode: Disadvantages

With such a varied number of possibilities it is very difficult to be specific about the disadvantages of group mode teaching. The most commonly recognised problem is that it may be expensive in terms of tutor time, but this depends on how it is organised. If the tutorial is dominated by the tutor, with little space for trainee interaction, then it indeed becomes an expensive and time-consuming form of informal lecture. We have seen how it is possible for a single tutor to organise a class as sub-groups which can interact with one another, with the tutor and with the group as a whole in various ways. Further, we may note that not all group work requires a tutor to be in attendance (peer-led groups). Indeed, it is a common experience that tongue-tied discussion groups can become quite voluble if the tutor finds an excuse to leave them for twenty minutes or so! This is especially the case where the members of the group perceive a wide gap in status between themselves and the tutor, or are apprehensive that the group interaction may be used as the basis for covert assessment. There are also forms of group work which require the trainees to collaborate outside class (project work is a common enough example).

A criticism of the group mode often expressed by trainees is that some sessions are aimless, with no perceived beneficial result for learning. Phrases such as 'just talking shop' or 'a pooling of ignorance' convey this feeling of nothing having been achieved in the learning process. There are two possible explanations for this kind of evaluation. The first explanation is that nothing has, in fact, been achieved or learned. There are many possible causes of this: the tutor, for example, may have held the tutorial, etc. purely as a matter of routine and has not thought out what form of learning outcome she anticipates from it. The second possible explanation of the trainees' poor evaluation of a tutorial is that they have learned something from it, but are not aware of what it is they have learned. For this reason, the closure of a discussion session, for example, can be very important. It is usually worthwhile establishing a brief summary of the main issues that have been raised and resolved (if they have been resolved). It is also useful if these main points can be recorded in some way, as this gives them added substance.

A common reason for the failure of group work, which is not always articulated, or even recognised, by the participants is that there is some malfunctioning in the personal relationships within the group. There is a tendency (particularly in language teaching) to see group work as *per se* an unproblematic activity once the organisational side of it has been sorted out. There is also almost a conspiracy in higher education to pretend that group work (seminars, etc.) is only about ideas, and feelings don't enter into it. Neither of these propositions is true, as anyone who has worked extensively with groups will know. Overcoming these problems requires, first, a recognition that they exist, and secondly the intellectual and emotional honesty to bring things into the open and deal with them. To do this effectively demands sensitivity, and perhaps some self-development, on the part of the tutor. (In some universities and colleges it has been found useful to set up self-development groups of tutors to develop awareness of this affective dimension of group work in an experiential way. For a very helpful study of these issues, see Bramley, 1979.)

PERSONAL REVIEW

Have you experienced any problems about being a member of a learning group in the past? What was the nature of the problems? How were they resolved? How would you resolve them now (either as a member of the group, or as a leader of it)?

3.8 Evaluation

Whatever mode of teaching and learning is used, its success cannot be taken for granted. Even something which is very successful with one group of trainees may not work with another group who may have seemed very similar. It is therefore most important to evaluate the teaching and learning that is taking place. One of the important aspects of evaluation is testing, but it is clearly not the only one. Examination success cannot be the only criterion for the success of a programme in educational terms: this is particularly the case where (as usually happens in higher education institutions) the examinations are set and marked by the institution itself. Other formal and informal methods (discussions, questionnaires, and so on) monitoring the 'health' of the course should be used. These important topics have only been touched upon here, and will be dealt with at greater length later.

Summary

In handling the 'received knowledge' areas of the teacher education curriculum, it follows from the previous chapter that there ought to be a varied and flexible approach involving a range of teaching and learning techniques. For teacher education, these techniques ought to feature in various ways the following key aspects of the academic process: acquisition, reflection, application and evaluation. Both the lecturing and the group teaching modes can fulfil a wide variety of teaching and learning purposes. All modes carry certain inherent advantages and disadvantages and thought should be given as to how to maximise the former and minimise the latter.

PERSONAL REVIEW

Have you ever been present at a very good lecture or group session? What was it that made the lecture or group session successful? How far can these aspects be applied to other lectures or group sessions, or were they particular and specific to that situation?

Glossary of some common modes of teaching and learning in higher education

(Note: this is a VERY SELECTIVE list. You may find it useful to keep a note of any other reading and learning modes that you come across.)

BRAINSTORMING

A kind of group activity intended to generate a lot of ideas. Participants are encouraged at the beginning to think up ideas no matter how unlikely or far-fetched. Every suggestion is recorded. Decisions about practicality are made later.

BUZZ GROUPS

A form of group activity in which groups of students have a brief discussion (for, say, five minutes) to generate ideas, answer specific questions, etc. Sometimes used as an activity during LECTURES *(see* GAPPED LECTURE*).*

CAL

See COMPUTER ASSISTED LEARNING.

CASE STUDY

A group activity which uses the data generated by a real 'case' or typical professional situation. The case study may use actual documents from the case, e.g. a syllabus, letters, reports, etc.

COMPUTER ASSISTED LEARNING

A method of learning which involves the use of specially designed computer programmes. Often abbreviated to CAL.

CROSS-OVER GROUPS

A form of group activity in which the class is divided into groups which have a discussion. After some time, one or more members of each group move over and join one of the other groups. So two students from Group A might join Group B, two from Group B might join Group C, and so on, and the discussion continues. In this way, ideas from the different groups are shared without the need for a FEEDBACK SESSION.

DISTANCE LEARNING

A system whereby students can have access to learning materials even when they are remote from the college, university, etc. which produced the materials. Students may be kept in touch by correspondence, radio, television, etc.

ELICITATION

See SOCRATIC TECHNIQUE.

FEEDBACK SESSION

A class activity in which various individuals or groups report back to the class on what they have been researching or discussing. It may also mean a session in which a tutor reports back to students with an evaluation of their work (e.g. after an assignment has been corrected).

FIELD STUDY

A kind of TASK-BASED *activity which involves studying phenomena at first hand. Popular in environmental sciences such as Geography or Botany because observations can be made in their natural setting. School observation is a kind of field study.*

FORMAL LECTURE

A kind of LECTURE *which is often carefully prepared in the form of a paper or script which is closely followed. Usually audience participation is not welcomed except perhaps for questions at the end.*

GAME

A kind of SIMULATION *which usually involves elaborate rules and decisions about who has been successful and who has not.*

GAPPED LECTURE

A kind of LECTURE *which is interspersed with other types of activity, e.g.* GROUP WORK.

GROUP WORK

Any form of learning activity which is done by groups of learners working together. Often distinguished from class work, in which the whole class works together.

GUIDED READING

A form of teaching or learning in which students are encouraged to read specific articles or specific sections of books with a particular purpose in mind.

INFORMAL LECTURE

A kind of LECTURE *which is delivered informally. Usually this means that audience reaction during the lecture is welcomed.*

JIGSAW LEARNING

A form of teaching or learning in which different students cover different areas of a topic; they later pool their knowledge (e.g. by means of SEMINAR *papers).*

LECTURE

A system of teaching where a tutor talks to the students for an extended period of time (usually between 45 minutes and one hour). Essentially one-way inter-action, but there are many variations. See FORMAL LECTURE, INFORMAL LECTURE, LECTURETTE, GAPPED LECTURE.

LECTURETTE

A shorter than usual LECTURE *(e.g. 15–20 mins). Sometimes given by individual students to the other members of the class, to share information and/or demonstrate presentational skills.*

OPEN LEARNING

A system whereby students can have access to learning materials (usually specially designed materials) at times which are convenient to themselves, in order to complete a programme of study.

PROJECT

A kind of TASK-BASED *activity which usually involves an extended amount of independent work, either by an individual student or by a group of students.*

PYRAMID GROUP

A form of group activity in which the class is divided into groups. After some time, pairs of groups are joined together and continue the discussion. This procedure is repeated until there is only one group, comprising the whole class. Sometimes called a SNOWBALL GROUP.

ROLE PLAY

A form of SIMULATION *in which the participants adopt certain roles or parts, e.g. Head-teacher, Parent, Student, etc.*

SELF-HELP GROUP

A group of students who come together to help one another, outside the official tutorial or teaching system.

SEMINAR

A form of group activity in which one or more, and perhaps all, of the participants has to contribute something to the discussion, usually in the form of a prepared paper or talk.

SIMULATION

A group activity which imitates (simulates) situations, usually those which are likely to arise in one's real-life professional activities. May sometimes involve ROLE PLAY.

SNOWBALL GROUP

See PYRAMID GROUP.

SOCRATIC TECHNIQUE

A form of teaching by question and answer gradually leading to the elicitation of certain truths. Used by Socrates, a Greek philosopher.

TASK-BASED (LEARNING)

Used to describe any kind of learning which involves the performance of a specified task or piece of work.

TUTORIAL

A form of group activity, usually led by a tutor. Tutorials may take a whole variety of forms, e.g. WORKSHOPS, *discussions, etc. Sometimes tutorials may be held on a one-to-one basis (i.e. one tutor, one student).*

TUTORLESS GROUP

Virtually a kind of SELF–HELP GROUP *but officially recognised. It operates without the benefit of a tutor or teacher, who may, however, be available as a resource.*

WORKSHOP

A kind of TASK–BASED *group activity which involves the completion of a certain specified task. It is expected that all the members of the group will contribute something to the completion of the task.*

4 Relating theory and practice: The reflective model

4.1 Overview

This chapter picks up the central question of relating theory to practice which was briefly discussed in Chapter 1. It attempts to provide a framework for thinking about the relationship betw⌄. theory and practice, various elements of which will be filled out in more detail in the chapters which follow.

4.2 The reflective model

The first part of this chapter will be concerned with elaborating the 'reflective model' of professional education and/or development presented in Chapter 1. That model was deliberately simplified to keep it in line with the discussion at that stage. In this chapter, an expanded and slightly modified version of the model is presented, and this version is summarised by the diagram in Figure 4.1.

It will be seen from Figure 4.1 that the process of professional education/development has been divided as follows:

Stage 1: The pre-training stage, i.e. the stage which the person who has decided to undertake professional training or development is at before beginning that process. The 'trainee' may be pre-service, or may already be engaged in the profession (in-service or self-development).

Stage 2: The stage of professional education or development.

Goal: What the professional aspires to, namely (increased) professional competence.

Each of these will now be discussed in turn. It must be stressed that the model is intended to apply to both pre-service and in-service education/ development, although no attempt will be made to follow through those distinctive applications systematically, on the grounds that it is potentially tedious and hopefully unnecessary for the majority of applications.

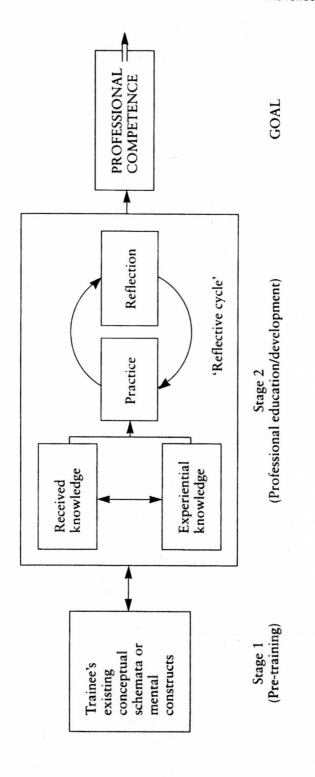

Figure 4.1 Reflective practice model of professional education/ development

4.3 Stage 1: Pre-training

This stage has been inserted to show more clearly the contrasting points of departure between this model and the 'applied science' model previously presented. In that model, there is a tendency, all too often realised in practice, for the primary agent of professional knowledge to be seen as someone other than the trainee, for example, an academic researcher or 'expert'. In the 'reflective model', the place of such agents is tacitly acknowledged (in that they are the generators of 'received knowledge'), but the 'reflective model' deliberately highlights the trainees and what they bring to the training/development process.

The 'reflective model' therefore emphasises the fact that people seldom enter into professional training situations with blank minds and/or neutral attitudes. This is especially true of the profession of teaching, where the trainees have been exposed to the practice of the profession, either willingly or unwillingly, during their most impressionable years.

What is it, then, that the trainee brings to the training/development situation? It has been argued that the number and complexity of professional decisions made every working day by teachers (and presumably the same applies to other professionals) is such that they cannot be explained only in terms of the conscious application of specific, taught 'skills'. Nor can professional action be entirely random or ad hoc: if it were, it would obviously be incompetent. MacLeod and McIntyre (1977:260) explain the phenomenon of the complexity and immediacy of professional decision making in terms of a certain limited number of deep underlying 'conceptual schemata' or constructs of what appropriate professional action might be. (Here 'construct', as I interpret it, is being used as a broad term to include a cluster of related concepts such as ideas, beliefs, attitudes, etc. all of which shape our behaviour in various typical or consistent ways.)

Thus, for example, language teachers who have detected a learner making a pronunciation error in the target language will usually deal with it in a way that is at least partly determined by mental constructs of the type just described (i.e. in the light of their views on the importance of fluency as opposed to accuracy, on the nature and cause of the error, appropriate ways of dealing with such errors, the importance of pronunciation errors as opposed to other kinds of errors, and so on). Of course their reaction may also be influenced by aspects of the incident specific to this particular situation: their relationship with a particular learner, whether they are feeling particularly tired or irritable at the time, etc. But, in general terms, if they are competent professionals, they will exhibit an overall consistency of response in this area which will relate to the repertoire of mental constructs which they have developed.

Such schemata or constructs will obviously be more important and probably more clearly defined in the minds of experienced professionals than in the minds of those new to the profession, whose constructs about professional action (such as they are) will not have been so dearly won, perhaps over many years.

It is perhaps feasible to subdivide 'conceptual schemata' into those which have derived from what has been read or taught, on the one hand, and those derived from professional experience on the other, but it is not clear what would be gained from such an endeavour. Over time, the sources of such constructs may become obscure even to the person who possesses them. Sometimes action precedes intellectual discovery: I have occasionally been thanked by in-service teachers at the end of a talk because I have provided an intellectual justification for what they have been doing anyway! In any case, the sources of mental constructs are probably many: personality factors, social factors, cultural factors and many others would have to be taken into account. To put it simply, I would say that while it might be useful to find out where trainees are 'coming from', it is vital to find out where they are 'at' now; and I would stress that no training or supervisory procedures can function with maximum effectiveness without this information.

PERSONAL REVIEW

It has just been suggested that a teacher's typical behaviour is largely determined by certain broad but deeply held 'conceptual schemata' or 'mental constructs'. Either for yourself, or in discussion with colleagues, discuss your conceptual schemata, in this sense, in relation to some or all of the topics which are listed below. For example, with regard to (a), you might ask yourself how important you think this is; what causes it; what is the most effective way of overcoming it; how much of it is the student's 'fault', and how much the responsibility of the teacher, the coursebook, the syllabus, or whatever.

a) Persistent grammatical errors in students' essays
b) The occurrence of a pronunciation error of the 'ship/sheep' variety
c) The value of group work
d) The importance of a lot of student talk
e) The purpose in teaching the target language in your context
f) The importance of getting the whole of the syllabus covered
g) What the important factors are that are conducive to student motivation

---

Once you have decided what your position is, pick a few of the items and ask yourself how your professional action as a teacher would be changed if you held different views. Would it make a significant difference, or not? If it would, how?

4.4 Stage 2: Professional education/development

In this stage, two key elements are highlighted: 'received knowledge' and 'experiential knowledge'.

Received knowledge As we have previously established, by 'received knowledge' we mean facts, data, theories, etc. which are either by necessity or by convention associated with the study of a particular profession.

You will notice in Figure 4.1 that the two elements in Stage 2 are linked by a vertical reversed arrow, which may be taken to symbolise a close, reciprocal relationship. It is a corollary of this model that the 'received knowledge' element should both directly inform the 'experiential knowledge' element and be directly informed by it. This is a very important but difficult requirement, and it will therefore be convenient to postpone discussion of it until after the 'experiential knowledge' element has been dealt with in isolation.

Experiential knowledge Giving this element its due emphasis, and exploiting it to maximum advantage, is at the very core of the 'reflective model'. The 'experiential knowledge' referred to is mainly the 'experiential knowledge' of professional action (practical experience). This is not to deny the importance to any professional of other kinds of experience gained from the 'University of Life', of course; however, since this is a model of professional education/development it is professional action which has to be the major experiential focus.

It might be objected that not every course has space for practice sessions. Some in-service courses may consist simply of a series of inputs of various kinds: in other words, they may operate entirely in the area of what I have called here 'received knowledge'. The effectiveness of such courses will obviously depend on how well they relate to the trainees' own 'reflection' and 'practice'. In other words, the trainees (the in-service teachers) may evaluate the inputs in terms of their own practice and either decide to change their teaching in some way, or not. If they incorporate the new techniques (or whatever) in their subsequent practice, they may then reevaluate them in the light of that practice.

This is probably the normal course of events with in-service courses of that type. In this way, the process of 'reflective practice' takes place, albeit that the action of practice takes place outside the formal framework of the course.

To take a concrete example, a teacher may go to a talk on reading comprehension, and come across the technique of asking pre-questions before reading a passage for comprehension. The teacher may relate this to the sort of mental constructs which she has about reading, and may decide that it is a technique worth trying. After the talk, she may try it out on her class and, if she is pleased with the way that part of her lesson has gone, she may incorporate this technique into her repertoire of techniques for teaching reading comprehension.

This is a very common way in which professional competence is developed, and in it the process of 'reflective practice' is clearly taking place, even though the actual practice element occurs outside the formal framework of the 'course'. This use of practice is obviously valid, and is perfectly in keeping with the model under discussion, yet at the same time it has to be recognised that this use of practice for professional education carries certain disadvantages.

The main disadvantage is that the experience is private, not shared. The articulation of it is consequently anecdotal, for example, as in comments such as, 'That would never work with my class', 'I tried it and it worked like a dream', etc. Since the data are private and individual the whole authority of the evidence derives from the speaker, and consequently from the speaker's credibility. Reflective discussion is very difficult or is at least based on an insecure foundation.

A second problem is the potential lack of focus in the discussion. Why would the technique not work with a given class? What aspects of it would not work? What does it mean, exactly, to say that it 'works like a dream'? In the absence of first-hand data (primary data) available to all those present at the discussion, such questions may be seen as an attack on the teacher's authority as an interpreter of her own experience.

A third problem could well be the lack of structure in the mode of articulating reflection. Susan Knights has emphasised the importance of disciplined listening in one-to-one situations where the participants take it in turn to think aloud without interruption. She argues that ' . . . talking through one's ideas with the thoughtful attention of another person is a powerful way of clarifying confusion, identifying appropriate questions and reaching significant heights' (Knights, 1985:90). Similarly, David Walker has argued for the importance to reflection of writing, particularly using a special kind of workbook which he calls a 'portfolio'. He suggests that, among other things, ' . . . it provides an objectivity in relation to the initial learning experience. It can clarify the original experience by removing from it clouds of subjective feeling that can obscure it' (Walker, 1985:63). Whether or not one is enthusiastic about any particular technique, it is clear that it is the experience of some that a structured mode of articulating reflection can sometimes lend significance and permanence to what otherwise might be trivialised and/or forgotten.

This is not to downgrade personal experience which, especially with experienced teachers, is usually most valuable. However, it does suggest the complementary importance of shared experience of practice in teacher education courses at all levels, and in discussion of such practice being focussed along selected parameters.

The nature of this shared experience can be very varied. More and more TEFL courses are making use of commercially available videos of samples of teaching, of which *Teaching Observed* and *Teaching and Learning in Focus* (British Council) are good examples. The main problem with such films is that they are not seen as relevant to viewers outside their own immediate context (Tomalin, 1988). Microteaching, transcripts of lessons, observed teaching practice, and so on are other ways of providing shared experience which can then be used as data for reflective dialogue. As the importance of such data for professional education/development becomes clearer, so practice tends to occupy a more prominent and central position in teacher education.

By and large, practice is valuable for professional education and development to the extent that it is reflected upon. Unreflective practice is not without value, of course. The simple act of teaching day after day can develop self-confidence, and make the teacher feel more at home in her profession, but it is essentially a consolidating function. Development implies change, and fruitful change is extremely difficult without reflection. The unthinking or rote application of innovation is an invitation to disaster. All too often, teachers attempt an approach or technique which has been reduced to a formula, with obviously no understanding of the rationale of the method or technique being used or its application in the particular context. The teacher has not been given, or has not taken, the opportunity to think the thing through, and to think it through in terms of her own context.

The issue of reflection does not only relate to whether or not it takes place, but also to the quality of the reflection. Improving the quality of reflection in professional education and development must be a major aim of the 'reflective model' and the problem of how to achieve this will be one of the main themes of succeeding chapters.

The relationship between 'received knowledge' and 'experiential knowledge' So far these two elements have been discussed largely in isolation, although the point has been made that 'received knowledge' inputs can be taught and learned more 'experientially' by using appropriate techniques.

To clarify the discussion, it might be worthwhile to list some of the topics which might appear under the heading of 'received knowledge' in a pre-service teacher education course for, let us say, Teaching English as a Foreign Language:

Description of the English Language
Linguistics
Psychology of Learning
Psycholinguistics
Sociolinguistics
Educational management and administration
TEFL methodology

(It should be emphasised that the subjects in the above list are merely examples: the issue of course design is one which will be discussed in more detail in Chapter 9.)

How are we to relate these subjects to the periods of teaching practice and/or school experience? An extreme 'applied science' approach would be to teach the subjects in their own right and then expect the trainees to apply somehow the findings of these areas of knowledge to their teaching situation. They might be given some help in doing this in the Methodology classes (if the Methodology lecturer actually knows what is going on in those other inputs). The 'reflective model' argues for a totally different approach. If at all possible, ways should be found of making the relationship reciprocal, not one-way, so that the trainee can reflect on the 'received knowledge' in the light of classroom experience, and so that classroom experience can feed back into the 'received knowledge' sessions.

There will be detailed exemplification of how this has been done in the case study which is discussed in Chapter 9. At this point, we might note that at least four aspects of the course will have to be examined carefully:

1. Is some, at least, of the school experience or teaching practice organised and timed in such a way that it can feed into the 'received knowledge' subject sessions and also be influenced by them?
2. Is there any timetabled period when tutors delivering 'received knowledge' inputs can meet with trainees to discuss the inputs as related to the trainees' school experience?
3. Is the assessment of the 'received knowledge' inputs organised in such a way that trainees have an opportunity to display their ability to apply 'received knowledge' in a school or classroom context?
4. Is there any machinery of course organisation which allows the 'received knowledge' subject tutors to harmonise their inputs so that they can see, at least partially, how these inputs relate to one another, as well as to school experience?

We should be clear about what is being proposed here. If it is the case that 'Linguistics' or 'Education', or whatever, is being pursued purely as an academic discipline in its own right, then there is no reason why it should have links with any other part of the course. If it is the case, however, that the justification of such subjects is that they are supportive

c

of professional education and development in terms of practice, then the course design should be explicit about how this putative relationship is going to be implemented and evaluated. Experience of teacher education courses shows that there is little gain in leaving it 'up to the students' to make their own application. For one thing, students have a natural tendency to 'compartmentalise' knowledge which is received in different learning contexts and from different tutors. Secondly, the application of academic information to practice is usually a fairly sophisticated operation, which most trainees cannot achieve without guidance.

The 'reflective cycle'   The 'reflective cycle' is a shorthand way of referring to the continuing process of reflection on 'received knowledge' and 'experiential knowledge' in the context of professional action (practice). Of course, this reflection may take place 'before the event'. As we are reading texts or listening to lectures, etc. we may well be reflecting on such inputs and understanding them *with reference to our professional concerns*. Reflection may also take place by a process of recollection: as we struggle with a professional problem or dilemma we recall relevant knowledge or experience that may help us with our evaluation of the problem. Or finally, it may take place during the practice itself: 'reflection-in-action'. The point that is being highlighted by Figure 4.1 is that it is the *practice* element which is the central focus of the knowledge base on the one hand and the reflective process on the other.

The teacher as researcher   It has been recommended by some writers that the process of reflection should be formalised, as it were, and that the classroom teacher should also become a researcher. This, of course, would help to undermine the dichotomy between theory and practice which has been identified as an unfortunate but typical consequence of the 'applied science' model. There are real problems: to do research properly requires special expertise, a lot of time, financial resources, and even perhaps particular personality traits, for example, an academic bent, etc. It may be that not many teachers will share all these interests and advantages, especially the provision of time and financial resources. In this respect, it has been suggested that teachers might be more interested in a type of research which is more under their own control and which might also be more relevant to the classroom, i.e. what is often called 'action research'.

The main criterion for 'action research' is that it should be addressed to practical problems and should have practical outcomes. The term therefore covers a wide range of possible research techniques and findings. For teachers who regard conventional research as not for them, 'action research' can be attractive for two reasons:

1.   It can have a specific and immediate outcome which can be directly related to practice in the teacher's own context.

2. The 'findings' of such research might be primarily specific, i.e. it is not claimed that they are necessarily of general application, and therefore the methods might be more free-ranging than those of conventional research.

There is an increasing amount of documentation of case histories of 'action research' (see, for example, Hustler et al, *Action Research in Classrooms and Schools*, 1986). In that book Bassey has a useful article in which he describes 'action research' of the limited and specific kind that has just been described, which he calls the 'study of singularities' (Bassey, 1986:21). Bassey shows how it might be possible, by a limited degree of careful observation and by some reflection, for teachers to modify their practice. He uses an imaginary example of a teacher who regularly finds queues of children at her desk with consequent time-wasting. Data gathered might include: How many children? (measured at regular intervals); Which children? (any particular children more frequently in the queue than others?); Why? (a codified record of each child's reason for being there). The children are involved in collecting the data, and when it is analysed, certain steps are taken which shorten the queues (and the improvement is measured).

'Research' of this kind is simply an extension of the normal reflective practice of many teachers, but it is slightly more rigorous and might conceivably lead to more effective outcomes.

PERSONAL REVIEW

Look at three or four of the following areas, and decide how you would organise a simple piece of 'action research' which might assist your reflective practice in the target areas. Remember that your approach does not have to be very 'rigorous' or 'objective'.

a) A teacher settling into a new school, who is particularly concerned about forming good relationships with her new colleagues.

b) Group work. A teacher who is worried about the quality of the target language in a group when she is not directly supervising it.

c) A teacher who is intrigued by the issue of how errors are corrected, especially in her own practice.

d) A teacher who wants to know what strategies her students use when they are confronted with a word whose meaning they do not know.

e) A teacher who is disappointed at the level of motivation and student involvement in a voluntary adult education language class.

4.5 Goal: Professional competence

The term 'professional competence' can be used in two senses. In one sense it is the indication, in some formal way, that someone has met certain minimum requirements for the exercise of his or her profession. Thus one's competence to teach might be proved by a certificate gained at the end of a teacher education course many years ago. In this sense, 'professional competence' is a fixed hurdle; once it has been successfully passed over, there is no going back on it except in very exceptional circumstances. Let us call this professional adequacy 'initial competence'.

There is another sense of 'professional competence' in which it is, as it were, a moving target or a horizon, towards which professionals travel all their professional life but which is never finally attained. The variables are many: society's expectations; the nature of the subject; the examination system; the school curriculum; methodology; the teacher's own interests; the teacher's changing and deepening insights into the nature of the profession; changes in responsibility, etc. Competence here has come a long way from 'adequacy' or even 'proficiency': it has the stronger force of 'expertise'.

Viewed from this perspective, professional certification (in whatever form it might take) is not a terminal point but a point of departure. (In Figure 4.1, this is indicated by the continuing arrow from the final box.)

If the second sense of 'professional competence' (i.e. expertise) is as valid and important as the first, then it is clear that equipping trainees with the techniques to go on developing competence in that sense must be an important secondary goal in any trainee's programme. (It is not the most important goal, of course: that would be, as it was always intended to be, to make trainees competent in the first sense, which I have called 'initial competence'.) We will therefore expect that ways of measuring the competence of one's own practice (self-evaluation), techniques of looking at one's practice as objectively as possible, techniques of using sources of self-improvement, and so on, will all figure in a complete programme of professional education and development.

4.6 Summary

In this chapter, the elements of the 'reflective model' of professional education and development have been examined in some detail, as have the relationships between these elements. In particular, we have seen the importance of relating what the trainees bring to the course and what they gain during the course. We have also seen the importance of breaking down the barriers between 'received knowledge' and 'experiential knowledge'. Finally, we have considered the importance of the continuing cycle of practice and reflection which leads to a dynamic, developmental concept of 'professional competence'.

PERSONAL REVIEW

By yourself, or in a group, make a note of any problems that bother you in language teaching, or simply aspects of practice that you would like to know a bit more about. In the same way as with the previous 'Personal review', see if you can work out forms of 'action research' which you could do (a) on your own or with minimal help, and/or (b) with a certain amount of funding and a reasonable amount of free time.

---

5 Classroom observation: Recalling and analysing the data

5.1 Overview

In the last chapter, a model for professional training or development was presented, the core of which was a 'reflective cycle' involving professional action ('practice') and reflection on that action. In this chapter I will suggest that the reflective process can be facilitated in two important respects. The first respect is in terms of how the professional action can be recalled so that it is available for reflection. The second respect is in terms of how the professional action can be most fruitfully analysed as part of the reflective process. The chapter finishes with a substantial 'Personal review' section which brings together various aspects of the chapter in relation to a short lesson transcript.

5.2 Recalling and analysing professional action

The most immediate problem in the discussion of this topic is that there exists a vast array of approaches and techniques in relation to the analysis of professional action, a full account of which would require much more space than is available here. In this chapter, therefore, a rather selective 'broad brush' approach will be adopted which will attempt to highlight techniques and approaches which might be most helpful to teacher educators, supervisors and teachers involved in their own professional development.

Those who would like detailed knowledge of how observation systems work are recommended to follow up the suggestions for further reading which are listed on page 167.

5.3 Key parameters

It will be seen from Figure 5.1 that four 'key parameters' are presented for consideration. They are: 'primary data', 'medium', 'interpreter' and 'interpretation'. Of these, the first two ('primary data' and 'medium') are concerned with answering the question: How can we recall the data of

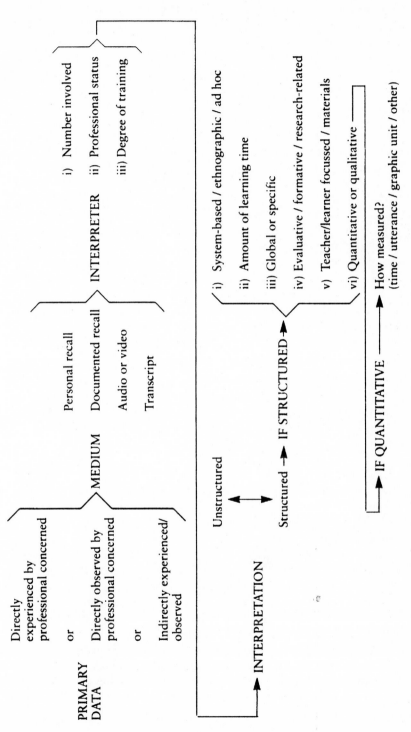

Figure 5.1 Some key parameters in the recall and analysis of professional action

professional action? The second two ('interpreter' and 'interpretation') are concerned with answering the question: How can we analyse the data that has been recalled?

In what follows, each of these key parameters will be considered in turn.

Primary data

By 'primary data' we mean the actual events of the professional action: what really happened. As John Fanselow has pointed out (Fanselow, 1977), recalling 'what really happened' is no easy task. It is a problem which has long fascinated artists, and Fanselow makes reference to the Japanese film *Rashomon* (directed by Akira Kurasawa) in which four characters involved in a rape-murder give different accounts of 'what really happened'. Fanselow makes the point that 'when teachers, supervisors, employers, students or sales people discuss the same lessons, texts, tests, methods and schools of language teaching, they often sound like the characters in 'Rashomon' – they each give contradictory or equivocal accounts of the same events or items' (Fanselow, 1977:17). It is clear, therefore, that a dialogue between, say, a supervisor and a trainee about a lesson runs the risk of being vacuous, unless both parties can agree first on what happened: the primary data.

In Figure 5.1, three sources of these primary data are listed:

1. Professional action is directly experienced by the professional concerned, in other words, the teaching to be analysed has been done by the trainee or in-service teacher, etc. who is concerned with the analysis. Clearly this perspective is unique and extremely valuable in any account of 'what really happened'.
2. The professional action is directly observed, i.e. by someone who was present in the class when the original class took place. This kind of observation is also extremely valuable, since certain aspects of the action will be clear to the observer in a way that they cannot be to the teacher. (In sport, there is the old saying that 'The spectator sees most of the game!')

    There is also the possibility of tapping into the teacher's personal experience of the action by conversation before and/or after the lesson.
3. The professional action is indirectly experienced or observed. This is what occurs when, for example, we watch a teaching film that has been professionally produced. Such films can be invaluable for training purposes, but we sometimes feel frustrated because, firstly, we have to view the action through the producer's eyes, and secondly, we have no opportunity to interact with the teacher or the students directly. Also questions we might wish to ask are

sometimes left unanswered, such as 'Was the lesson rehearsed?',
'Did the students already know what they were going to be taught?',
and so on.

Medium

The most common forms of recall are listed below, in ascending order of
'technical difficulty'.

It should be noted that it is, of course, possible for the same events to
be recorded through more than one medium. In a microteaching class,
for example, a teaching episode may be discussed by a group of trainees
who have access both to their own recollection of the teaching and also
to a video of the same microlesson.

1. **Personal recall**   This is the simplest form of recall, where the
    teacher and/or observers of the lesson simply try to remember what
    they can of the professional action, and carry out their reflection on
    that basis. This may be linked to, for example, interviews with a
    sympathetic outsider who helps the professional to articulate her
    experiences. (For an interesting example of this, albeit not related to
    language teaching, see Elbaz, 1983.)

2. **Documented recall**   Here the recall is aided by a document of some
    kind. It may be just a written account of the lesson as it is observed
    or remembered. Perhaps the simplest and most flexible approach
    here is in the form of field notes or teaching diaries (see Hopkins,
    1985:59, 60). There may be an 'observation schedule' of some kind
    which helps to focus recollection (observation schedules will be
    discussed at greater length when we come to discuss interpretation).

3. **Audio**   This is the simplest form of electronic recall. It can be
    surprisingly effective, especially if one is primarily interested in the
    teacher's input, or in small-group interaction (see, for example,
    Wallace 1981a).

4. **Video**   At one time considered very 'high-tech', the use of video is
    daily becoming more commonplace. Its use can vary from involving
    a studio, technicians and several broadcast-quality cameras on the
    one hand, to using a simple hand-held camera with playback
    facilities on the other.

5. **Transcript**   A transcript is a verbatim account of the interaction
    that has occurred in a lesson, or in a part of a lesson. In one sense,
    therefore, it is simply a very full kind of 'documented recall', as
    described above. However, transcription has been placed last here
    because most transcripts actually derive from an audio or video
    record of a lesson. Sometimes the transcripts are handwritten by a

trained observer and subsequently typed up. Producing a transcript can therefore be a fairly complex and time-consuming process. The great advantage of transcripts is their accessibility: it is usually easier to make a detailed analysis of a transcript than from an electronic (audio or video) recording. (For some imaginative uses of transcripts in TESOL teacher education, see Brown, 1988, and Ramani, 1987.)

The interpreter

Once the data are made available, by whatever means, the next question is: Who has the responsibility for interpreting the data? Here again there are various possibilities: (1) the number of interpreters, (2) the professional status of the observer, and (3) the degree of training.

1. **Number of interpreters** All too often, there is only one: the teacher herself. If she wishes to have a reflective dialogue with someone else, the teacher has to give her interpretation of her professional action to, say, a colleague. The colleague then has to give what advice she can on secondary data, i.e. at second hand, as it were. In a microteaching class, on the other hand, there will be several 'interpreters', including perhaps a supervisor, and even 'students' if the microlesson has been with a peer group. This is one reason why microteaching can be such a powerful technique for professional development.
2. **Professional status** In the case of a reflective dialogue or discussion, the status of the participants in the discussion may be very important. A reflective dialogue with a fellow trainee who has observed one's lesson may be very different from that with a supervisor or a student in the class.
3. **Degree of training** This may be related to professional status. Obviously, the chances are that a supervisor who has observed hundreds of lessons is more highly skilled in observation than someone who is new to the profession. However, there is also another kind of specific training, which relates to a particular method of observation. As we shall see later, some methods of teacher observation are highly technical and, in that sense, a trainee fresh from college who has been taught these techniques may be more highly 'trained' in that aspect of observation than a much more experienced fellow professional.

PERSONAL REVIEW

Have you ever done any of the following?

1. Listened to colleagues discussing their teaching
2. Sat in on a colleague's lesson
3. Watched a video or film of someone teaching
4. Read a transcript of a lesson, or part of a lesson

What would you say were the advantages and/or disadvantages of each of these different ways of sharing someone else's teaching experience?

The interpretation

How professional action is interpreted by an observer may vary along a cline from being almost completely unstructured at one extreme to being very highly structured at the other. An example of an almost completely unstructured observation might occur when a visitor to a school is invited to watch a class in operation. The visitor may have no ideas at all about what to look for, nor any criteria for analysing the interaction that he or she observes. (Even in such a situation, of course, there is some degree of structure, in terms of the preconceived ideas and expectations which the visitor, however unsophisticated, will bring to what ought to be going on in a classroom.) At the other extreme, the observation may be very highly structured indeed, as we shall see.

Some ways of structuring interpretation

A few minutes' thought will reveal that the number of ways in which interpretation might be structured is open-ended. At its most basic, structuring interpretation is not a sophisticated technique, but something which we must do every waking minute in order to make sense of the sensations that we are aware of. Cognitive psychologists have argued for some years now that reality is 'constructed' out of the raw material of the senses, according to certain mental 'frames' or 'schemata' which are imposed on the sensory input. (For a useful survey of how this approach is applied to language, see Greene, 1986, throughout, but especially pp. 33–50.)

In this section, we shall be looking at some categories of interpretation which seem to be very relevant in the present context, but others are possible. The categories for interpretation that we shall be looking at deal with whether the approach to interpretation is:

1. System-based, ethnographic or ad-hoc
2. Requiring learning time (how much?)
3. Global or specific
4. Evaluative, formative or research-related
5. Teacher-focussed, learner-focussed or neutral in focus
6. Quantitative or qualitative

It will be clear in the discussion which follows that some of the oppositions which have been set up here are not as clear-cut as they might appear. For example, observation instruments which are primarily evaluative may also be used for formative (i.e. training) purposes, and vice versa. It will also be clear that the six sets of categories listed here overlap in various ways. Nevertheless, in spite of these 'grey areas', it has been my experience that these are the categories which surface whenever observation systems are discussed with fellow professionals, and therefore it seems worthwhile to attempt to tease out these distinctions here. The first set of distinctions (system-based, ethnographic or ad-hoc) is the most complex and you might therefore find Figure 5.2 useful as a point of reference for what follows.

1. SYSTEM-BASED

'Bellack Tradition' (Bellack, 1966)
    e.g.   Sinclair and Coulthard: 'Classroom discourse analysis' (1975)
             Fanselow: 'Focus' (1977; 1987)
             Bowers (1980)

'Flanders Tradition' (Flanders, 1970)
    e.g.   Wragg (1974)
             Moskowitz: 'FLint' (1971)

Other LT Observation Systems
    e.g.   Mitchell and Parkinson (1979)

2. ETHNOGRAPHIC

    e.g.   described by:
             Stubbs and Delamont (1976)
             Hammersley and Atkinson (1983)

3. AD-HOC

    Many examples, e.g. Wallace (1981*b*), Kerry and others (1981), Perrott (1982), Ramani (1987), Brown (1988).

Figure 5.2   Some structured approaches to classroom observation

5.4 System-based observation

By system-based observation we mean that the observation is based on a
system of fixed observation categories. The system usually has a 'brand
name' as it were, very often in the form of an acronym. Many hundreds
of such systems have been produced, but the two most influential have
been the one devised by Bellack and others (1966), and the one devised
by Flanders (1970). We shall therefore begin by briefly commenting on
these two systems.

1. **BELLACK and others (1966)**   Curiously enough, Bellack and his
    colleagues do not seem to have used an acronym to name this
    system, perhaps because they were among the first to analyse
    systematically what took place in classrooms. They did this by audio
    recording fifteen high school teachers and 345 students in classes
    studying a unit on international trade. The recordings were then
    made into verbatim transcripts, which were typed in a standardised
    way, i.e. so many letters to a line, etc. This meant that the classroom
    interaction could be reliably measured by counting lines. So, for
    example, you might find that a teacher would talk for twenty lines
    of the transcript and the student's response would take up three
    lines, and so on.
    The interaction was also categorised according to certain
    observation categories which were arrived at by careful examination
    of the data. The full system of categories is very complex, but two
    specific aspects of the system proved to be very influential. The first
    noteworthy aspect is the discovery of four basic pedagogical moves,
    namely:

    STRUCTURING MOVES, which are used for organising or
    contextualising what follows, e.g. 'I am going to start by asking
    you a few very easy questions.'
    SOLICITING MOVES, which are intended to elicit a response from the
    student, usually (but not always) in the form of a question, e.g.
    'What is the plural of the word *child*?'
    RESPONDING MOVES, which take the form of responses to soliciting
    moves, e.g. 'The plural of *child* is *children*.'
    REACTING MOVES, which are caused by a previous move but are not
    elicited by them. A very common type of reacting move is when a
    teacher praises or comments on a student's answer.

    The second aspect of the process which Bellack and his colleagues
    explored was the fact that moves fell into common teaching cycles.
    For example, a very common teaching cycle is STRUCTURE – SOLICIT
    – RESPOND – REACT.

Thus, we have:

What was said	Type of move
T: I am going to start by asking you a few very easy questions.	STRUCTURING
T: What is the plural of the word *child*?	SOLICITING
S: The plural of *child* is *children*.	RESPONDING
T: Good!	REACTING

2. **FLANDERS (1970): FIAC** Unlike the system of Bellack et al, the Flanders system was intended to be used while the teaching was actually in progress. It may have been Flanders who popularised the fashion for using acronyms to denote observation systems: FIAC is an acronym for 'Flanders Interaction Analysis Categories'. Flanders' system consists of ten categories (Flanders, 1970:34). Of the ten categories, seven are used to categorise various aspects of 'teacher talk' and two are used to categorise 'pupil talk'. The last category is used when there is 'silence' or 'confusion' in the class, i.e. when there is no interaction to record or when there are so many things going on that the observer is not sure what to record.

Of the seven categories relating to teacher talk, the first three are concerned with how the teacher responds to the pupils by: (1) *accepting feelings or attitudes* expressed by a pupil; (2) *praising or encouraging* a pupil; or (3) *accepting or using pupils' ideas*. The fourth teacher category relates to *asking questions*. It will be seen that in these four categories the teacher is either responding in a positive way to the pupils or interacting with them. These are sometimes called 'indirect' behaviours.

The last three teacher-related categories are: (5) *lecturing*, where the teacher expresses or explains her own ideas, or gives information which she has selected to the pupils; (6) *giving directions, orders, commands*, etc. which the pupil is expected to obey; and, finally, (7) *criticising or justifying authority*, for example, when disciplining a pupil who has misbehaved. These are sometimes called 'direct' behaviours.

The two 'pupil talk' categories are: (8) *pupil-talk response*, for example, answering a question; and (9) *pupil-talk-initiation*, for example, when pupils volunteer some ideas of their own or ask a question. As we have noted before, the last category is: (10) *silence or confusion*.

FIAC uses a pencil and paper technique for recording the interaction. A trained observer sits at the back of the class and at regular intervals (usually about every three seconds) categorises the interaction he or she has just seen in one of the ten categories. An example of a completed tally sheet has been provided by Flanders (1970:38) and is reproduced here (see Figure 5.3). You might like to

look at the totals and reflect on what light they throw on this
particular lesson.

Category number		Completed tally marks made by an observer	Total tallies	Per cent
Teacher	1	III	3	0.8
	2	THL I	6	2.5
	3	THL THL II	12	5.0
	4	THL THL THL THL II	22	9.2
	5	THL THL THL THL THL THL THL THL THL THL THL THL THL THL THL THL THL THL THL THL THL THL THL THL THL THL	130	54.2
	6	THL THL THL I	16	6.7
	7	IIII	4	1.6
Pupils	8	THL THL THL THL II	22	9.2
	9	THL THL II	12	5.0
Silence	10	THL THL IIII	14	5.8
		Total	241	100.0

Figure 5.3   Flanders' FIAC system: Completed tally sheet (Flanders, 1970)

5.5 Observation systems of special relevance to language teaching

In what follows, we shall look at some observation systems which are, or may be, especially relevant and useful for observing language teaching (LT) classes: we shall call them 'LT Observation systems'.

Observation systems commonly used tend to be similar either to the model provided by Bellack and others, or to the model provided by Flanders (although this is by no means the whole story: see Croll, 1986, for a very thorough survey). We shall therefore, as a kind of shorthand, talk about the 'Bellack tradition' and the 'Flanders tradition'. In the 'Bellack tradition' we might note: (1) the fact that the data are measured from a *transcript*, i.e. the data have to be first recorded and then transcribed, and (2) the central place of labelled units of discourse ('moves') such as structure/solicit/response/reaction. In the 'Flanders tradition', on the other hand, we have a form of *documented recall* (see page 63), in which twenty or so tallies may be made every minute under one of a range of categories: in other words, the preliminary analysis is done in 'real time' as the lesson is proceeding.

LT Observation systems: The Bellack tradition

Three interesting systems which can be related, to a greater or lesser extent, to the 'Bellack tradition', will be considered here. They are:

1. Sinclair and Coulthard's 'Classroom discourse analysis system' (see Sinclair and Coulthard, 1975; Coulthard, 1977).
2. Fanselow's 'Focus system' (see Fanselow, 1977; 1987).
3. Bowers' system for tabulating interaction in foreign language instruction (see Bowers 1980 *a*, *b*).

SINCLAIR / COULTHARD SYSTEM (1975)

This system is a form of discourse analysis which is especially concerned with *classroom discourse*. Its primary thrust is therefore *linguistic* rather than *pedagogic*, although its designers have argued, with considerable justification, that it can have some very useful teaching applications. Taking their cue from systematic grammar, Sinclair and Coulthard argue for a *hierarchy* of observation categories (analogous to the hierarchies found in grammar, where a SENTENCE consists of CLAUSES, which consist of PHRASES, which consist of WORDS, which consist of MORPHEMES). So we have a similar hierarchy for a lesson:

Lesson Hierarchy

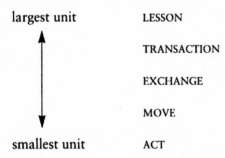

largest unit	LESSON
	TRANSACTION
	EXCHANGE
	MOVE
smallest unit	ACT

As the uppermost limit, a LESSON is marked by some observable marker that the lesson is beginning or ending (just as a sentence is indicated by a capital letter at the beginning and a full stop at the end). A TRANSACTION is a major stage of the lesson which is marked linguistically by characteristic expressions and intonation patterns such as 'Right', 'OK then', etc. An EXCHANGE is a sequence of MOVES (rather similar to Bellack's 'teaching cycle'); so an 'eliciting exchange' input goes like this (Coulthard, 1977:106):

ELICITING EXCHANGE		
Move	**(Discourse)**	**Act**
Initiating	T: Can anyone have a shot, a guess at that one?	Elicit
Responding	P: Cleopatra.	Reply
Follow-up	T: Cleopatra. Good girl. She was the most famous queen, wasn't she?	Accept Evaluation Comment

It will be seen that, whereas for Bellack and his colleagues, the MOVE was a basic unit, the more sophisticated linguistic analysis of Sinclair and Coulthard subdivides the MOVE into ACTS, as indicated above.

FANSELOW (1977; 1987)

Fanselow's approach derives from his conviction that teachers (and supervisors) are controlled most of the time by 'invisible rules' that they are unaware of, and his system is intended to reveal what these 'rules' are. His approach seeks to explore all the possible relevant dimensions along which changes can be made in teaching behaviour. His approach is therefore multi-dimensional. He lists 'five characteristics of communication' as follows:

1. Who/what communicates with whom?   (*Teacher, student(s), material*)
2. What is the pedagogical purpose of the communication? (*Structure, solicit, respond, react*)
3. What mediums are used to communicate content?   (*Linguistic, non-linguistic, part-linguistic, silence*)
4. How are the mediums used to communicate content?   (*Attend* – e.g. by listening; *characterise* – e.g. by labelling parts of speech; *present* – e.g. by reading aloud; *relate* – e.g. by making generalisations; *re-present* – e.g. by paraphrasing)
5. What areas of content are communicated?   (*Life* – i.e. things related to real life such as greeting the pupils; *procedure* – i.e. dealing with organisation, etc.; *study* – i.e. the subject matter of what is being studied, etc.)

By first of all coding what we are doing along the various dimensions, Fanselow believes that this consciousness gives us the power to change our professional action in various controlled ways.

BOWERS (1980)

Bowers' analysis is concerned with characterising patterns of classroom discourse and investigating the efficiency and effectiveness of the various patterns of discourse.

Bowers expands the Bellack moves from four to seven as follows: (1) *Responding*; (2) *Sociating* (i.e. concerned with maintaining relationships); (3) *Organising*; (4) *Directing* (i.e. any act which encourages a non-verbal activity as an integral part of the learning task); (5) *Presenting* (information, ideas, etc.); (6) *Evaluating*; (7) *Eliciting*. He applies these categories both to 'teacher talk' and 'pupil talk'. He also takes note of when the target language (TL) is used. An interesting aspect of Bowers' system is that it allows him to make the interaction graphic by means of a kind of flowchart. In the following extract, the children are English-speaking and the TL is French. The teacher is trying to elicit the meaning of the phrase *on va tarder un peu* (= we're going to be a bit late). The oblique line (/) indicates a pause.

		Category of move
T:	On va tarder un peu/	(Eliciting)
P1:	What's tarder mean	(Eliciting)
T:	Tarder/what's tard mean/	(Eliciting 2)
P:	Late	(Responding)
T:	Late, so tarder the verb would mean	(Evaluating; Eliciting)
P:	Later	(Responding)
T:	To be/late/	(Presenting)
P2:	Going to be late	(Presenting
P1:	They're going to be late	(Responding)
T:	Yes, they're a bit late	(Evaluating; Presenting)

This could be displayed as in Figure 5.4 (adapted from Bowers, 1980*b*:86–7). The diagram shows the pattern of interaction and it also shows graphically how little of the interaction is in the target language – basically only the first utterance.

LT Observation systems: The Flanders tradition

Some investigators have been attracted by the advantages of the Flanders approach (e.g. it can be done in 'real time' and does not require a transcription; it gives the appearance of being very 'objective', and so on), but found that it did not address aspects of interaction of particular interest to them. Foreign language teachers are usually interested to know, for example, how much of the interaction is in the target language. They may wish to know if a 'pupil response' (category 8) is a group response (as in a choral drill) or an individual response, and so on.

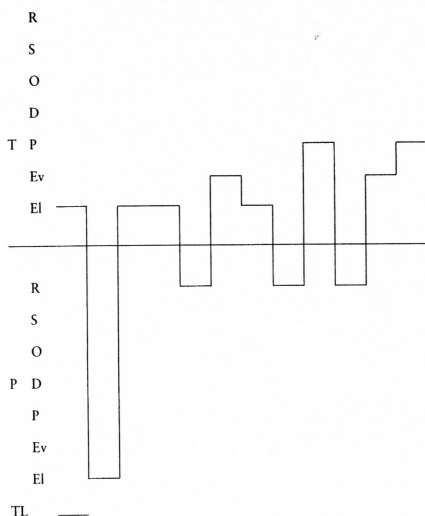

Figure 5.4   Graphic display of classroom interaction

Wragg tried to make the Flanders system more suitable for analysing the foreign language classroom simply by doubling the number of categories, resulting in a twenty-category system: 'Categories 11 to 20 are the same as Flanders 1 to 10 but are used when interactions occur in the foreign language' (Wragg, 1974:100).

THE FLINT SYSTEM (MOSKOWITZ, 1971)

The acronym 'FLint' stands for 'Foreign Language Interaction' analysis and was devised by Gertrude Moskowitz, as an aid to foreign language teachers for self-observation. It is a more complex system than FIAC, and Moskowitz recommends that teachers should master FIAC first (Moskowitz, 1971:214).

The functions of the extra categories in FLint are to record:

1. Whether the teacher uses jokes
2. Whether the teacher uses a response verbatim
3. Whether the teacher corrects 'without rejection' (i.e. without blaming the pupil)
4. Whether the teacher directs pattern drills
5. Whether the student response is individual or choral
6. Whether a period of silence is related to the use of audio-visual equipment or not
7. Whether 'confusion' (FIAC's category 10) is work-oriented or not
8. Whether there is laughter or not

Furthermore, there are two 'subscripts' (i.e. small letters put at the bottom of the category numbers) which tell us:

1. Whether the interaction was in the target language or in the native language
2. Whether there is evidence of non-verbal gestures or facial expressions by the teacher or the students which communicate without the use of words (in which case the small letter *n* for NON-VERBAL is added to the category number)

It will be seen that some of Moskowitz's extra categories reflect matters of interest to all teachers; others might be said to reflect a particular methodology (the concern with audio-visual aids and with choral response); and others (e.g. categories concerning jokes, correction without rejection) might be related to the writer's particular interest in the affective atmosphere of foreign language classes (see Moskowitz, 1978).

Other LT Observation systems: Mitchell and Parkinson (1979)

It has already been noted that not all systems can be ascribed to the Bellack or Flanders 'traditions'. One interesting approach which steps outside these traditions is that devised by Mitchell and Parkinson (1979; described in Malamah-Thomas, 1987:60–2). Like Fanselow's system, it is also multi-dimensional, with five main dimensions:

1. Topic (civilisation, general linguistic notions, etc.)
2. Language activity (interpretation, drill, exercise, etc.)
3. T-mode (i.e. Teacher mode: instructing, working with group, etc.)
4. P-mode (i.e. Pupil mode: listening, speaking, reading, etc.)
5. Class organisation (whole class, individuals doing the same task, individuals doing different tasks, etc.)

Interestingly, Mitchell and Parkinson suggest that the categories should be applied to segments of a lesson rather than single utterances: we are dealing with a much more flexible unit of measurement here.

Advantages of systems using fixed observation categories

It will be remembered that, in this chapter, we have been concerned with observation as a necessary step for reflection on experiential knowledge rather than as a basis for academic research (received knowledge). In what ways can system-based observation aid professional reflection? The following points could be made.

Systems using fixed observation categories (e.g. Bellack, Flanders):

1. *Objectify* the teaching process; providing data which a teacher and a supervisor can agree on as to what 'really happened', *within the particular categories that are utilised by the system.*
2. Provide a *reliable* record: some studies show that trained observers using a particular system can demonstrate a very high level of agreement among themselves; (see Borich and Madden, 1977:449).
3. Promote *self-awareness* in the teacher, by the very act of using them.
4. Provide a *meta-language*, which enables teachers to talk about their profession in a more appropriate way because they have a shared *technical language.*
5. May make teacher training more *effective* by improving the *quality of teaching* (see, for example, Moskowitz, 1968).

Disadvantages of systems using fixed observation categories

Fixed observation systems of the kind we have been describing have not been without their critics, one of the most notable critiques being in *Explorations in Classroom Observation* by Stubbs and Delamont (1976), from which most of the points listed below are taken.

Some important criticisms of fixed observation categories are:

1. Most of the systems ignore the *temporal and spatial context*, e.g. there is usually very little discussion of the physical setting.
2. The *boundaries* between the categories may be crude or ill-defined.
3. The emphasis on *quantification* may be excessive. As Dunkin and Biddle have pointed out (1974:353): ' . . . perhaps the greatest single flaw in much of the research we have received is the persistent assumption that appears to underlie much of it – that teaching can somehow be reduced to a scalar value that can be indicated by a frequency for some teaching behaviour. We suspect, with Taba, that this is simply not true.'

4. The systems use *pre-specified categories*: ' . . . category systems may assume the truth of what they claim to be explaining' and, further ' . . . by placing arbitrary (and little understood) boundaries on continuous phenomena may create an initial bias from which it is difficult to escape' (Stubbs and Delamont, 1976:9).
5. The *concerns* and the social and pedagogical assumptions of the designers *are built into the systems*.
6. Most of the systems do not concern themselves with the teacher's (or the students') *intentions*.
7. In practical terms, most of the systems are extremely *time-consuming* either to learn or to use, or both, and are therefore unlikely to be used by practising teachers.

5.6   Ethnographic approach to observation

In an attempt to overcome the perceived disadvantages of the kind of 'fixed system' approach we have been discussing so far, a different approach has been suggested which has been variously described as 'ethnographic', 'ethnomethodological' or 'anthropological'. Hammersley and Atkinson (1983:2) describe the method thus: ' . . . for us ethnography (or participant observation, a cognate term) is simply one social research method, albeit a somewhat unusual one, drawing as it does on a wide range of sources of information. The ethnographer participates, overtly or covertly, in people's daily lives for an extended period of time, watching what happens, listening to what is said, asking questions, in fact collecting whatever data is available to throw light on the issues with which he or she is concerned.'

It will be seen that this is a much more open-ended approach, where the observer first identifies areas of concern (without necessarily pre-determining what those might be), and devises what kind of data collection might seem appropriate.

It should be noted that, while advocating what they call the 'anthropological' approach, Stubbs and Delamont (1976) are refreshingly modest about its potential. They dissociate themselves from 'the congenital and manic optimism with which much educational research is suffused', and they deplore 'the pursuit of short-term reliability at the expense of long-term validity', while emphasising the usefulness of an 'exploratory or heuristic stance'.

PERSONAL REVIEW

Imagine it has been decided to make an ethnographic study of how group work operates in language teaching at a given level in any teaching situation that you are familiar with.

1. Who do you think would be best suited to conduct such an investigation? Someone, like yourself, who is familiar with the situation or someone to whom the situation is 'strange' (perhaps someone from another school or college, or an adviser or inspector, etc.)?

2. How many days or weeks do you think would be necessary to complete the study?

3. What activity would be necessary outside the lesson? Interviews with the head-teacher/principal or head of department; the examination of syllabuses, etc.; interviews with teachers or students; the examination of students' workbooks, etc.?

4. What form of data would be collected inside the classroom and how would it be collected? Would video or audio recordings be used? What about seating plans? How would the group work be observed? Would it be better to concentrate on one group or on several? Would you analyse the data from the group(s) according to a system, or according to what turned out to be interesting?

5. If everything went according to plan, how *generally* useful do you think such a study might be?

5.7   Ad-hoc approach to observation

Both the system-based approach and the ethnographic approach would seem to be unwieldy from the point of view of the practising teacher. There seems to be a case for an approach to observation which is flexible and eclectic, in that it will use both quantitative and qualitative data where each seem appropriate. It seems rather pretentious, and even somewhat misleading, to term this approach 'ethnographic' since it will not necessarily (or even usually) have that sense of entering a culture for an 'extended period of time' which Atkinson and Hammersley have characterised as the job of the ethnographer (see above). It seems better to go for a more modest title, which is why it is simply being called here 'ad-hoc', i.e. devised for a specific purpose (whatever that purpose might be). Unlike the fixed category systems we have been discussing, in this approach, it is assumed that each different area of concern will yield a different system of analysis. We have already noted that the fixed systems we have been examining are not necessarily inflexible, and we have indeed discussed many modifications of them for various purposes. (See, for example, the interesting way in which Bowers has adapted his approach to suit the 'ad-hoc' needs of a particular group of trainees in Bowers, 1987:158–179.) Obviously, however, such flexibility must have limits, and the observer has to decide whether she prefers the convenience (and perhaps reliability) of working within an established system, or the freedom to observe the phenomena through the focus of an entirely ad-hoc system.

I have described elsewhere (Wallace, 1981*b*) how such a system might be arrived at in a training (or self-observation) situation. The approach described is basically a guided 'discovery' approach in which the trainers devise their own observation system. Let us suppose, for example, that a teacher wanted to reflect on techniques for the elicitation of vocabulary meaning. It would not be difficult to set up a situation where a group of students are faced with a passage containing some unknown words (this could even be done artificially by leaving blanks or using nonsense words). The teacher would tape record her elicitation of the target vocabulary. At the end, the tape would be played back, and the teacher (or supervisor in a training situation) would simply stop the tape from time to time and ask the question 'What is happening here that relates to the target skill?'

The use of this technique in one training situation established the following 'meta-language' to denote various stages of elicitation: FOCUSSING (i.e. directing attention to the target word, or a part of the context); CONTEXT (i.e. use of the context to aid inference); BACK-GROUND KNOWLEDGE (i.e. exploration of background knowledge as an aid to inference); INFERENCE (i.e. a direct attempt to elicit or infer the target meaning). Certain commonly used sequences were established, e.g. FOCUS–BACKGROUND KNOWLEDGE–FOCUS–INFERENCE. It is this kind of detailed 'nitty-gritty' expertise, usually taken for granted by the experienced practitioner, which is often ignored in training situations, and sometimes has to be learned in the field by trial and error. The main benefit is not the data 'discovered' by this small piece of action research (for that is what it is), but the opportunities for detailed, focussed, data-based reflection on an important area of language teaching, and the provision of a meta-language with which to discuss it.

For an example of a very simple ad-hoc observation schedule related to questioning procedures in reading comprehension, see Figure 5.5.

QUESTIONING: READING COMPREHENSION TEXT

1. Put a tick (✓) for each time the teacher asks one of the
    following types of questions, and add up the total of ticks
    (tallies) at the end.

    Type of question   Tallies   Total
    ----

    a) LITERAL (simple retrieval of
        information from the text)
    ----

    b) INFERENTIAL ('reading between
        the lines')
    ----

    c) REORGANISATIONAL (combining
        information from different areas
        of the text, e.g. summary)
    ----

    d) EVALUATIVE/REACTIVE (expressing a
        judgement or personal reaction)

2. Have you any comments on the distribution of questions
    under categories (a) – (d)?

3. How many times did the teacher:

    a) not get a response?   Tallies .... Total ......

    b) get a wrong response? Tallies .... Total ......

    How did the teacher deal with such responses?

4. Was there any significant question which the teacher might
    have asked but didn't?

Figure 5.5   Sample 'ad-hoc' observation schedule

PERSONAL REVIEW

1. Look at the ad-hoc observation schedule in Figure 5.5.

    How useful might such a schedule be to a trainee teacher or a teacher listening to or watching a tape of her lesson?
      What problems do you anticipate in the use of this schedule? For example, will it be clear to everyone exactly what is meant by the term 'question'? Are there other ways of getting responses apart from 'questions'? Should Bellack's term 'solicit' be used instead? Would you count repeated questions, etc.?
      Are there any other observation activities, apart from those used in the schedule, which you think it might be useful for trainee or in-service teachers to perform in this area of questioning and reading comprehension?

2. Pick an area of teaching that you think would benefit a trainee to observe carefully (e.g. blackboard work, group work, dealing with errors, presenting a structure, etc.).
      See if you can devise a simple observation schedule which might help someone observing a piece of teaching in that area. (If you have access to a sample of teaching in the target area on tape or in transcript form, you can see how well your schedule works, and modify it as necessary.)

5.8   Fixed-system/ethnographic/ad-hoc: Summary

Perhaps it would be useful at this stage to take stock of what has been said so far about the general approaches to the observation of teaching that we have been discussing.

We dealt first with **fixed-system** approaches which used an established, fully worked-out system, and usually related to the work of a particular researcher or group of researchers. First, there are approaches in the '*Bellack tradition*', utilising transcripts and featuring labelling systems for units of discourse. Prominent in this tradition are the systems devised by: *Sinclair and Coulthard* (classroom discourse analysis, hierarchy of categories); *Fanselow* (multi-media); *Bowers* (distinguishing teacher moves and student moves under seven categories, use of target language is noted, can be expressed in flowchart form). Secondly, there is the '*Flanders tradition*' which can be done in 'real time' using a basic ten-category system, and has given rise to many variants, including: *Wragg* (twenty categories, distinguishing mother tongue and target language); *Moskowitz* (twenty categories and sub-categories, plus two 'subscripts' indicating use of mother tongue and non-verbal communication, emphasis on affective dimension). The possibility of other fixed-system approaches was noted, e.g. *Mitchell and Parkinson* (five main dimensions and more flexible units).

We then briefly looked at the **ethnographic** approach, which is usually non-quantitative and descriptive, but extremely flexible.

Lastly, we considered the **ad-hoc** approach, which is essentially an eclectic variation on the ethnographic approach, and which allows itself to use any means, quantitative or non-quantitative, to examine whatever seems relevant to reflect on professional action.

In the following sections, other parameters listed in Figure 5.1 will be looked at. This will be done briefly, since most of them have already been touched on in one way or another.

Choice of observation system

When faced with choosing (or devising) an observation system for generating data for reflection, the trainer, supervisor or teacher might ask herself the following questions:

1. Do I want a complete system which has already been worked out in detail, and is therefore 'ready made' as it were (in other words a *fixed system*)? Would I prefer to work out my own categories from in-depth observation, or perhaps use categories that have been devised by someone else to relate to a particular area of concern (*ethnographic/ad-hoc system*)?

2. How much *learning time* is involved? Can the system simply be picked up and used or does it need a period of training? If the latter, how long will it take me to master it? If I am going to devise my own categories, how long will that take? Is there any accessible source of observation instruments for the areas I am interested in? Can I easily adapt something that has already been published?

3. Am I interested in looking at the teaching *globally* (i.e. all aspects or a wide range of aspects) or at *specific* areas? (For some ideas on specific areas, look at some of the books in the excellent *DES Teacher Education Project Focus Books*, series editor: Trevor Kerry, and also Elizabeth Perrott's *Effective Teaching*.)

4. Do I wish to focus on the *teacher* or the *learner*, or on some *balance* between the two?

5. Am I interested only in *assessing* the classroom events, or am I more interested in *formative* (training) aspects, or am I interested in classroom data mainly for *research purposes?*

6. Am I interested in acquiring *quantitative* data (e.g. FIAC, etc.) or *qualitative* data (ethnographic approach), or in acquiring a mixture of both, as necessary (ad-hoc approach)?

7. If I am going to *measure* interaction how am I going to do it: by units of time, by graphic units (e.g. numbered lines on a page, etc.), by listing different kinds of utterance, or by some other method (e.g. labelling segments of a lesson)?

5.9 Conclusion

It ought to be clear by now that, whatever shortages there may be in educational provision, a shortage of observation instruments isn't one of them! Even so, it is worthwhile reminding oneself that this brief survey has merely scratched the surface.

It is obviously a 'buyer's market', but you may feel that the choice is overwhelming. How is one to proceed? The first thing is to be clear about what the data are required for: the *purpose*. When the famous mountaineer, George Mallory, was asked why he wanted to climb Mount Everest, he always gave the same answer: 'Because it is there.' This answer will not do for the use of observation systems on teacher education courses: there is no point in spending valuable course time on such systems simply because they exist.

We have established why observation of professional action is essential: it is through reflection on professional action that professional expertise is developed. How the reflection is structured is another matter. It may be that, for an in-service teacher, all that is required is a diary or some 'field notes' scribbled while a lesson is in progress. It may be that, for training purposes, a reliable, well-documented method (such as FIAC or its variants) is required, and time spent on learning to use it may be adjudged time well spent. It may be that the trainer will want to develop skill-specific observation schedules to tie in with, say, a micro-teaching programme. The trainer may, as I do, encourage students to identify problem areas and work out their own observation schedules, thus providing themselves with focussed data to reflect on. In such a scenario, it is worthwhile spending a few hours looking at different approaches to classroom observation, *not* with a view to mastering them, but simply to pick up ideas for one's own approach.

5.10 Summary

In this chapter we have looked at some key parameters in the recall and analysis of professional action. Various ways in which the primary data may have been examined or observed (either directly or indirectly) have been noted. Various kinds of medium for recalling primary data have been listed, for example, by video, by transcript, and so on. As far as the interpretation is concerned, it may be structured to varying degrees, and according to the basic approach being used by the observer. Here, two well-established approaches have been distinguished: a fixed system-based approach and an open-ended ethnographic approach. An eclectic ad-hoc approach to classroom observation has also been described. This is essentially a very simple and limited method of observation, which can be applied with little or no training.

PERSONAL REVIEW

What follows (on page 84) is a transcript of the first two to three minutes of a lesson. The tutor is intending to present the conditional form:

If I had . . ., I would have . . .   (e.g. If I had known you were coming, I would have prepared something for you.)

Please note that the lesson was never intended to be a 'model lesson'. It is simply a sample of a piece of typical teaching within a certain tradition. The lesson was taught in a UK language school to a small number of students at elementary level, all of whom are named in the transcript.

Read through the transcript, then attempt the following tasks:

1. Which of the following areas of teaching is there NO evidence of in the transcript?
   Questioning
   Class involvement
   Use of gesture
   Set induction (i.e. creating a situation where students are ready to learn)
   Reinforcement (i.e. encouraging or confirming correct responses)

2. What other areas of teaching is there EVIDENCE of?

3. *Quantitative analysis of interaction*   Various aspects of the interaction in the transcript can be quantified (counted or measured), for example:

How many questions were asked of each student?
Was the distribution of questions equal for each student?
What kinds of errors did the students make?
How did the tutor deal with these errors?
See if you can quantify the answers to these questions.

Are there any other aspects of the interaction that could also be measured? Make a list of them and either attempt to answer them yourself or (better) exchange them with someone else and ask him or her to answer them. Discuss any problems of measurement that arise.

4. *Qualitative analysis* Quantification on its own is often a pointless activity. The interesting questions arise from the analysis of the data that has been collected. In connection with this transcript, one might ask:

    What are the advantages and/or disadvantages of the tutor's
        questioning technique?
    Was there any *other* (not necessarily *better)* way in which the
        errors could have been dealt with?
    Can you think of any *other* (not necessarily *better)* ways in
        which this conditional form could have been introduced?

    You may care to think about these questions and compare your responses with others. Are there any other qualitative questions that could be asked about this transcript?

5. Think back to the various observation systems that have been discussed in this chapter. Which of them could be applied to this transcript? What sort of information would the various systems yield? How useful might this information be for a teacher trainee or in-service teacher?

6. What extra information about this teaching episode might a video or audio tape have given you? Do you think that extra information would have been worth the extra expense and time in making it available?

TRANSCRIPT
Initial presentation of a structure (Conditionals)

Tutor: Right, now I'm going to ask you some questions. I'd like you to answer them. Now, Jaffer, this morning, did you oversleep this morning? Did you oversleep this morning?

Jaffer:	Oversleep.
Tutor:	Can anyone help him with oversleep?
Jaffer:	Oversleep?
Tutor:	Sleep too long. Did you oversleep this morning?
Jaffer:	No, no I didn't. No, I didn't.
Tutor:	You didn't. Did you, Kyoko? Did you oversleep?
Kyoko:	No.
Tutor:	You didn't . . .
Kyoko:	I just got up early.
Tutor:	You got up early.
Kyoko:	Yes.
Tutor:	Right. What about you, Victor? Do you have an alarm clock?
Victor:	No, I don't have but my landlady comes and knocks at the door.
Tutor:	I see. So did you oversleep?
Victor:	No. Never.
Tutor:	This morning, did you?
Victor:	No, I didn't.
Tutor:	You didn't. How about you, Mariko? Did you oversleep?
Mariko:	No, I didn't.
Tutor:	You didn't.
Mariko:	I got up earlier than usual.
Tutor:	You got up earlier than usual.
Mariko:	Yes.
Tutor:	Good. Emad, did you bring your books and pencils to the lesson?
Emad:	Yes, I did.
Tutor:	What about you, Per? Did you bring your pencils, your books to the lesson?
Per:	Yes, I did.
Tutor:	You did. Now, Fusayo.
Fusayo:	Yes.
Tutor:	Did you fall down the stairs this morning?
Fusayo:	No, I didn't.
Tutor:	You didn't. What about you, Jaffer, did you?
Jaffer:	No, I didn't.
Tutor:	You didn't. Kyoko?
Kyoko:	No, I didn't.
Tutor:	You didn't. Did you run out of money last week, Emad? Did you run out of money?
Emad:	Yes, I did.
Tutor:	Ah. You did. Per, did you run out of money last week?

Per:	No, I'd money left.
Tutor:	You had enough money. I had enough money.
Per:	I had enough money.
Tutor:	OK, Kyoko, did you run out of money last week?
Kyoko:	Yes, I did.
Tutor:	I see, and what did you do?
Kyoko:	Oh, I bought a bus pass.
Tutor:	Pardon.
Kyoko:	Bus pass.
Tutor:	I see. You bought a bus pass. Ah, and what about you? Did you run out of money last week?
Student:	No, I didn't.
Tutor:	Naji, did you forget your glasses?
Naji:	I didn't.
Tutor:	You didn't. Did you forget your pens and books?
Naji:	No, I didn't.
Tutor:	You didn't. OK. Emad. Now, did you oversleep this morning?
Emad:	No, I didn't.
Tutor:	OK, so all of these things you didn't do. You didn't fall down the stairs. You didn't forget your glasses, forget your books. You didn't . . .
Student:	Run out of money.
Tutor:	Run out of money. You didn't . . .
Student:	Oversleep.
Tutor:	Oversleep. And Kyoko, did you oversleep?
Kyoko:	No, I didn't.
Tutor:	You didn't. You didn't. Right, now all of these things you didn't do. I want to know what you would have done if you had overslept.

6 Microteaching

6.1 Overview

The technique of microteaching will be presented in this chapter as one of a range of techniques for developing 'experiential knowledge' of professional action in a controlled and progressive way. Microteaching will be defined as a training context in which a teacher's situation has been reduced in scope or simplified in some systematic way. Various approaches to microteaching will be discussed, both in terms of its underlying philosophy and in terms of its implementation.

6.2 How knowledge of professional action is developed

We have seen that there are two ways of developing knowledge relating to professional action, each of which is complementary to the other and both of which are necessary. The first is by mastering the 'received knowledge' which is appropriate (or deemed to be appropriate) to the practice of the profession in question. The second is by acquiring, and reflecting on, 'experiential knowledge' of professional action itself. How is this experiential knowledge to be acquired?

Once more, it is useful to refer back to Schön's analysis of professional thinking and learning (Schön, 1983). Schön discovered certain constants which various practitioners brought to this reflection on professional action. One such constant was 'the media, languages and repertoires that practitioners use to describe reality and to conduct experiments' (1983:270).

One of the case studies which Schön analyses at some length takes place in a school of architecture, and shows how a master designer trains one of his students. In this particular case, the specific context is a design studio in which the students undertake a design project under the supervision of a master designer. The master designer and the students are concerned with certain skills, techniques, strategies, etc. relating to this aspect of their profession (i.e. the professional 'repertoires' in Schön's terms). In this learning context, the 'media' used are basically two: the spoken word (an open-ended dialogue between the master designer and the student), and the sketchpad on which both the master

D

designer and the student objectify their ongoing conceptualisation of the task. The meta-language which they use is the technical language appropriate to this kind of design: 'contour', 'layout', 'unit', 'scale', and so on.

It will be clear, of course, that this design studio is not a 'real' situation, in the sense that it is not exactly equivalent to what the student will be doing when he or she is a fully-trained professional. It is an artificial teaching environment. In spite of this artificiality, its usefulness is immediately apparent. One of the most important uses is that it allows safe experimentation. Designs of even large scale projects can be made, altered, or indeed completely scrapped at very little risk and at minimal cost.

We would therefore expect language teachers, like other professionals, to be provided with opportunities for safe experimentation while learning their profession, and, when qualified, for developing new skills and extending their professional repertoire. A range of such opportunities will be discussed in the next section.

6.3 Context of learning for language teaching trainees

There is probably no profession which restricts itself to only one kind of learning context for its trainees, and this must also apply to language teaching trainees. The range of contexts should be such that it can gradually bring the trainees from a position of minimum risk and cost, through increasingly realistic (and risky, and costly) contexts to the 'real thing', like this:

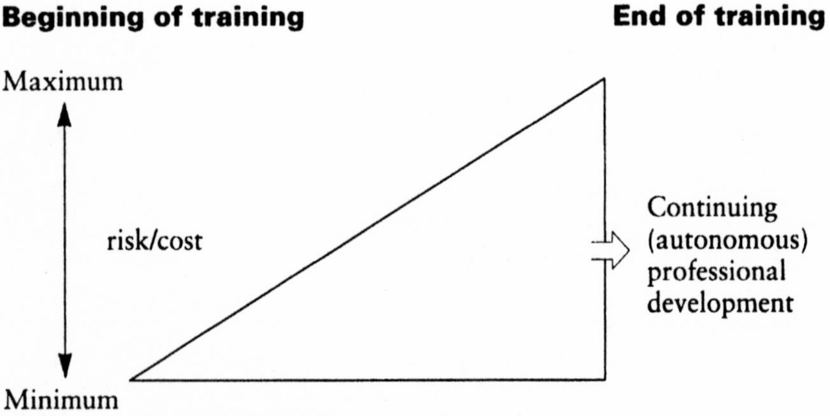

Beginning of training   **End of training**

Figure 6.1   Cline of learning contexts

It should be noted, perhaps, that the risk/cost factor is operational at several levels, of which we shall specify two here. The first is risk/cost to the client. It is obviously wasteful, and even harmful, for students to be taught by incompetent 'teachers', if that situation can be avoided. The second is risk/cost to the trainee. Let us take an extreme case, though by no means unknown, where someone with no training whatsoever is expected to stand up before a class and teach the students. The expectation is that by doing this such a person will learn how to become a teacher. The trauma of being thrown unprepared into a full classroom situation is not calculated to ensure any kind of rational professional development, and has probably on many occasions led to the choice of another career! (It is interesting to speculate why teaching is one of the few professions where this bizarre training procedure is even contemplated: perhaps because its usually disastrous consequences are not made a matter of public knowledge as speedily as in other more publicly accountable professions.)

In Figure 6.1, therefore, we have a model for a cline of learning contexts, allowing for varying degrees of safe experimentation. What are the various stages along the cline? In Figure 6.2, an attempt has been made to suggest some of the possible activities leading from minimum risk/cost activities at one end to autonomous professional action at the other.

The activities have been divided into various general categories, roughly corresponding to the amount of risk/cost involved in each type of activity. These categories have not been called 'stages', because use of that word would imply that once the trainee had moved on to a new type of activity, she would not return to a previous 'less risky' type of activity. This is clearly not the case. Observation of teaching films, for example, is an activity which a teacher might avail herself of at any stage in her career. However, such an activity will always be low profile and therefore relatively risk-free as far as the observing teacher is concerned.

6.4 General categories of training and teaching activities

1. **Data collection and analysis activities**   Many of these activities have been discussed in the previous chapter. They are obviously 'safe' and 'cheap' in the terms that we have been discussing, since the trainee has a mainly observational and analytic role.

2. **Planning activities**   Again, these are relatively risk-free, but a little more exposed since the trainee has to produce something that can be evaluated.

Degree of risk/cost	Activity	General category
Minimum	Observation / analysis of lessons on film	1. Data collection / analysis activities
	Observation / analysis of live taught lessons	
	Analysis of lesson transcripts	
	Draft exercises Draft lesson plans	2. Planning activities
	Microlessons (non-recorded)	3. Microteaching activities
	Microteaching (group preparation)	
	Microteaching (individual preparation)	
	Microteaching (peer group)	
	Microteaching (real pupils)	
	Extended microteaching	
	Supervised teaching	4. Supervised professional action
	Auxiliary teaching	5. Shared professional action
	Team teaching	
Maximum	Individual teaching (NB varying degrees of autonomy)	6. Individual autonomous professional action

Figure 6.2 Sample of training and teaching activities categorised according to putative risk/cost

3. **Microteaching activities**   These activities involve teaching short lessons exemplifying certain skills. The lessons are often video taped and discussed with one's fellow trainees. Here we are obviously on less certain ground. Some people would argue that microteaching is both a 'risky' and 'costly' procedure. It is risky, in that trainees or in-service teachers may be putting themselves up for possible criticism by their peers or colleagues, and/or supervisors. There are also costs involved, both in the hardware that may be used, and in the amount of time which microteaching absorbs, whether it is peer teaching or student teaching.

   As against these points, there are also ways in which microteaching can almost be a classic example of 'safe experimentation' in the gradual development of professional expertise. There are also ways in which material costs can be reduced and in which the risk of 'loss of face' can be minimised. These and other aspects of microteaching will be discussed more fully later in this chapter.

4. **Supervised teaching**   Again, it must be admitted that supervision can be a two-edged weapon. Approached wrongly, supervision can be a most threatening and demoralising experience. Approached properly (by both supervisor and trainee), it can be a relatively unthreatening, supportive and productive technique. Ways of handling supervision will be discussed in Chapter 7.

5. **Shared professional action**   This includes auxiliary teaching and team teaching. In *auxiliary teaching*, an experienced teacher has overall responsibility for the class, while an auxiliary teacher (perhaps a trainee) has some limited responsibility (e.g. for the functioning of a group of students within the class, or for a particular aspect of the lesson). In *team teaching*, the responsibility for the class is equally shared between two teachers (who may both be experienced, both trainees, or one experienced and one trainee). In both kinds of shared teaching, it is of course possible, though unusual, for more than two teachers to be involved.

6. **Individual autonomous professional action**   This is, of course, the most common teaching situation. The teacher operates as a fully-fledged professional in her own classroom. The teacher is to some degree independent or autonomous, in the sense that she is no longer a trainee, and therefore has to take personal responsibility for her professional action. However, the word *autonomous* might almost be put in quotes, since very few professionals are completely free agents, and this clearly applies to teachers also. The teacher is under various constraints from superiors, from colleagues, from the nature of the syllabus, from the textbook that is in use, and so on.

PERSONAL REVIEW

Look again at Figure 6.2. Which of the activities leading up to individual teaching would you regard as (a) essential, (b) desirable, and (c) irrelevant to a full programme of professional development?

6.5 Definition of microteaching

We have seen from the previous section that microteaching is in no sense a substitute for other kinds of professional experience. Rather, it takes its place along a cline of professional learning experiences, of which supervised teaching practice is probably the most important.

Let us therefore attempt to specify more narrowly what microteaching involves. (The description which follows is a slightly modified version of the one presented in Wallace, 1979:56.) As already noted in the Overview, microteaching denotes a training context in which a teaching situation has been reduced in scope and/or simplified in some systematic way. There are three main ways in which the teaching encounter may be scaled down:

1. The teacher's task may be simplified and made very specific.
2. The length of the lesson may be shortened.
3. The size of the class may be reduced.

Let us take these one by one.

1. **The teacher's task**   Usually the teacher is asked to practise only one 'skill' at a time. This skill is described to the trainee, usually by a tutor, with the intention that the trainee will know exactly what she is to do. The teacher is expected to concentrate on that skill. In some programmes, she is supposed to keep on practising the skill until she gets it right.

2. **The length of the lesson**   Since the teacher is concerned with only one skill there is no need for her to teach a full 40 or 45 minute lesson. In most programmes, the shortened lesson ('microlesson') lasts only five to ten minutes.

3. **The size of the class**   In a similar way, the size of the class may be reduced. Usually, a microteaching class is fewer than ten students, sometimes only four or five. The 'students' may be real students or fellow trainees.

6.6   Stages of microteaching

Microteaching is usually conceived of as occurring in three or four distinct stages. These are:

1. **The briefing**   This is the stage at which the trainee is given oral and/or written information on the skill she is to practise and the way it is to be done.

2. **'The teach'**   This is when the trainee actually teaches the microlesson. Sometimes the trainee teaches real students, and sometimes her fellow trainees ('peer teaching'). Where possible, the lesson is usually video taped.

3. **The critique**   This is the traditional name for the stage at which the trainee's microlesson is played back (if it is on tape), discussed, analysed and perhaps evaluated. It could well be argued that the term 'critique' is somewhat unfortunate because of its rather negative association with words like 'criticism' or 'criticise', and this is rather unhelpful since microteaching is usually intended to be a positive experience rather than a negative one. Perhaps terms such as 'analysis' or simply 'discussion' would be more appropriate.

4. **'The reteach'**   This is the final stage, but one which is not present in all programmes. In this stage, the trainee practises the same skill again in the light of the discussion in stage 3. In some programmes, the teacher is expected to continue practising the skill until she 'reaches criterion', i.e. until she has shown that she has mastered the skill.

6.7   Underlying concepts in microteaching

Microteaching may be related to two of the contrasting models of professional education which have been presented earlier, namely the 'applied science' model and the 'reflective' model. If this is done, then different implementations of microteaching as a formative technique are likely to emerge.

Microteaching and the 'applied science' model

The original development of microteaching as a teacher training technique at Stanford University was very much in the 'applied science' tradition. The theoretical basis for the Stanford approach was related, at any rate initially, to the psychological theory of behaviourism.

This is made very explicit in an article by Diana E. Bartley (Bartley, 1969) in which she relates the microteaching programme to immediate feedback, reinforcement, shaping and similar Skinnerian concepts, for example, 'Through successive approximations and corresponding rein-forcements, the intern's teaching behaviour gradually achieves accept-able standards' (*ibid.*:141). McGarvey and Swallow (1986:7) point out that the behaviour modification approach was strongly emphasised in the 'minicourse' model of microteaching developed by Borg and his co-workers at Berkeley University in California (see Borg et al, 1970).

The theory, therefore, was that the 'experts' would specify the skills of good practice. This would be conveyed to the trainees during their briefings. The trainees' behaviour would then be 'shaped' until they 'reached criterion'.

As McGarvey and Swallow have pointed out (1986:6), a list of teaching 'skills' were presented but 'no rationale or research evidence was presented to justify the focus on these particular skills'. Even researchers closely involved with the Stanford programme quickly became sensitive to the problem of specifying 'good teaching skills'. After describing an experimental programme involving the observation and analysis of the teaching of seventeen teachers of French, to discover 'good' and 'bad' language teaching behaviours, Politzer (1970:42) concluded: ' . . . the very high complexity of the teaching process makes it very difficult to talk in absolute terms about "good" and "bad" teaching devices'.

Another criticism of the isolated skills approach was that the effect of teaching is greater than the sum of its parts. Dunkin and Biddle (1974:353) remarked that: ' . . . it appears to us that any meaningful analysis of teaching behaviour *must* involve sequential elements'.

In view of their criticisms, it is not surprising that John Stoddart, in his thorough and perceptive review of microteaching practice in Britain with reference to TESOL, noted that: ' . . . none of the tutors using microteaching to whom I talked would seem to identify at all closely with the original Stanford aims based on a behaviourist rationale' (Stoddart, 1981:15).

Microteaching and the 'reflective' model

In discussing the 'reflective' model, the sheer complexity of the teaching process has already been commented on. Weller (1971:10), for example, has described teaching as 'a complex interaction of many poorly specified and little understood variables'.

MacLeod and McIntyre (1977:261) also comment on the complex nature of classroom teaching and have drawn some conclusions from this, as has been previously noted (in section 4.3). They suggest that a teacher's behaviour is *not* the demonstration of individual 'microskills' but of certain broad *schemata* or *constructs*, i.e. certain basic but powerful ideas which teachers relate their teaching behaviour to. For example, a decision about whether or not to discipline a student will probably relate to general ideas about what is appropriate student behaviour in various situations.

It is therefore suggested that it is more valid to see microteaching as a technique for professional reflection rather than simply as a technique for shaping behaviour. This is not to suggest, of course, that trainers should necessarily abandon their 'expert' status. It is generally true that most trainers welcome guidance and thrive on it. John Bright (1968), writing of his teacher training experience many years ago in the Sudan, mixed his metaphors to record how 'We saw the teachers blossom as they mastered the art of driving down the tramlines.' But, as Bright's account of his methods shows, he did not simply prescribe techniques: *he demonstrated their validity through experiential learning techniques.*

This is how Bright described one of his training techniques when he later taught at Makerere in Uganda: 'A volunteer was coerced into coming and [teaching], with the rest of the group doubling as pupils and critics. Anything could happen. It was useful to switch on a tape recorder at this point to know what did happen and thus to "objectify" the guinea pig. A recording made it easier for everybody, including the person who made it, to think about what happened and discuss it without personal involvement' (Bright 1968:21).

Bright is describing what might be called, in today's jargon, 'low-technology microteaching'. What is interesting is the very open-ended, exploratory and heuristic way in which teaching principles were arrived at, as when Bright got his students to make an analysis of pupil–teacher interaction in a language class in order to arrive at the concept of 'pupil practice'.

Having said all that, it is clear that the balance between prescription and freedom will differ from one situation to another. In some cases, firm direction will be both desirable and welcomed by the trainees. In others, a more open-ended approach may be advisable. Experience shows, however, that merely following instructions without understanding can lead both to meaningless teaching and to stunted professional development. If the findings of MacLeod and McIntyre are correct, then microteaching has potentially an important role in arriving at such an understanding.

6.8 Variations in microteaching

One of the advantages of microteaching is that it has proved to be an extraordinarily flexible technique. In the sections which follow, some of the components of microteaching will be looked at, especially in terms of possible variations.

6.9 General and specific programmes

The first decision to be made is whether to go for (a) a *general teaching skills programme*, or (b) a *subject-specific programme*. In (a), the microteaching programme will be handled centrally in a 'microteaching unit' (perhaps run by the department of psychology or education). In (b) the programme will be run by a particular subject department and taught within that department. The first alternative can be justified on economic grounds, but also on the basis of the existence of 'general teaching skills'.

However, many writers advocate a subject-specific approach. Andrews (1971:28) has argued that microteaching outside the sphere of any particular discipline can lead to 'a kind of skilful word-mongering in limbo'; further, 'each particular subject matter tends to generate its own kinds of treatment'. Johnstone (1977) points out some of the difficulties in creating a subject-specific programme (in his case, Modern Languages) related to a general skills programme. Some of the general skills specified, for example, higher-order questioning, were irrelevant to the level at which Modern Languages are mostly taught at Scottish schools. Another of the skills handled was 'Variation'; this led to a very varied microlesson on *avoir* (the French verb 'to have'), which was totally devoid of any attempt at contextualisation: so it was a good example of variation, but a bad example of microteaching! Such problems are not insuperable, of course, but there would seem to be a *prima facie* case for subject-specific microteaching where this is feasible.

6.10 Skills for microteaching

What are the teaching skills which are suitable for microteaching? Usually one thinks of microteaching as being more concerned with the interactive stage of teaching, rather than the pre-active (planning) stage. So, for example, lesson plans would not normally be part of a microteaching programme. We have to think therefore of 'skills' which are suitable for the microteaching format.

The concept of a 'skill' is in itself somewhat elusive. In some ways, its use is a relic of the behaviouristic approach which originally under-pinned microteaching.

Perhaps we could begin by noting the distinction between a *task*, which is simply something to be done, for example, 'teach the first five minutes of the very first lesson to a class of beginners', and a *skill*, in the sense of a technique which can be described and learned, for example, the orderly arrangement of information on a chalkboard. The performance of a task may be so tightly specified that it is indistinguishable from the performance of a skill, or it may be achieved by the use of various alternative techniques, or by a combination of techniques. The denotations of *task* and *skill* therefore overlap to some extent, but I hope the distinction is clear: a task is simply something to be done within the microteaching format; a skill can be described and/or modelled.

I have argued elsewhere (Wallace, 1979), that a distinction could also be made between *skills* and *strategies*.

Skills can be modelled reasonably easily, or specified in behavioural terms such as:

techniques of reading aloud,
use of visual aids,
variation in questioning,
redirecting questions,
organising group work, and so on.

Strategies are more cognitive (and possibly affective), and relate to how the teacher tackles certain recurring themes in language teaching such as:

the promotion and maintenance of learner motivation;
the place of errors and mistakes in language teaching, and how the
teacher should react to them,
the value of authentic communication and the ways in which such
communication can be brought about effectively,
the use of 'rules' and how they are presented, and so on.

In my experience, these are recurrent themes in microteaching programmes. They can hardly be described as 'skills', since they appear in a wide variety of guises and contexts. *Strategies* can be seen as relating *skills* to the 'broad cognitive structures' or 'schemata' which MacLeod and McIntyre (1977) speak of.

This kind of distinction seems to be supported, or at least complemented, by arguments put forward by McGarvey and Swallow (1986:154–5). Building on Hart's (1978) critical article 'Against Skills', McGarvey and Swallow make certain distinctions with respect to teaching performance. On the one hand, they recognise *performance skills* which are defined as ' . . . the technical, observable behaviours which constitute the teaching act and which can be adjudged to be performed skilfully'. On the other hand, they also recognise certain more complex 'skills', which, according to Hart, are not skills at all but human capacities. These capacities relate to two areas: *cognitive processes* and *affective learning*. There are therefore three dimensions to teaching ability which McGarvey and Swallow exemplify with reference to competence in a very common teaching process, namely EXPLAINING:

Performance skill: The teacher can present an explanation fluently and clearly.

Cognitive processes: The teacher can construct a rational explanation and can recognise suitable occasions to give explanations.

Affective learning: The teacher values explaining and wishes to give effective explanations.

The authors argue convincingly that microteaching programmes (and supervision programmes generally) would benefit from disentangling these three dimensions from the over-generalised use of the term 'skill'.

PERSONAL REVIEW

(a) Pick one of the teaching areas that are listed below. For the area you have chosen, try to think of up to six *skills* that it would be useful for a trainee teacher to be able to demonstrate. (If you are working in a group you could either concentrate on one area, or each member of the group could choose a different area.)

   Areas: 1. reading comprehension
   2. language function/structure
   3. vocabulary
   4. class organisation
   5. chalkboard work
   6. writing (composition)

(b) Now select *one* of the skills for the area you have chosen, and specify the actual *task* you would expect the trainee to perform in microteaching format. (You can take some things for granted, e.g. for (1) or (3) you can if necessary assume that you have found a suitable text for the trainee to work on.)

Keep a note of what you have done: it will be required for the 'Personal review' on page 99.

6.11 The briefing

The briefing may take the form of an oral discussion or a set of written instructions prior to the teach. Another source of variation in the preparation for microteaching is modelling: whether a model is presented or not, and, if presented, what kind of model is used. A distinction is usually made between *taped* or *filmed* models (which could also be on audio tape; video taped models are usually rather opaquely referred to in microteaching literature as 'perceptual models') and *transcript* models (i.e. transcripts or printed descriptions of model microlessons, usually referred to as 'symbolic models').

Research on modelling was surveyed by Turney and others (1973). They concluded, listing several studies, that 'There is now ample evidence that the careful use of models of teaching does produce significant student learning.' Some tutors, however, object to modelling on methodological grounds. Stoddart (1981:26) notes that tutors on UK TEFL programmes tended to avoid giving demonstration lessons, arguing that this might encourage students that there is simply a 'right' way to teach. However, one tends to agree with Stoddart that there does seem to be a case for offering trainees, especially very inexperienced ones, some kind of *sample* of what teaching might look like in a given situation.

PERSONAL REVIEW

Please look again at what you did for the 'Personal review' on page 98.

In about 50–100 words, write a *briefing* for the skill you have chosen there, explaining to the trainee the salient features of the target skill. Since you may find this quite difficult, feel free to tackle it in any way that seems appropriate to you. For example, you could stick to describing the performative aspects of the skill or you could take into account the cognitive and/or affective dimensions of the skill as well.

6.12   Preparing the microlesson

The preparation of the microlesson can be the responsibility of an individual trainee, or else it can be a joint undertaking with a pair or group of trainees. In the latter case, a group of trainees can prepare the microlesson together, and one member of the group volunteers to teach the lesson. The members of the group can act as 'guinea pigs' for a dry run of the lesson before the actual 'teach', which of course would be done with a different group. This system has many advantages as a learning experience, but does pre-suppose a reasonable degree of group cohesion. Generally speaking, microteaching should not be attempted with a group until they have had an opportunity to get to know and trust one another. (Kenneth Cripwell used games to develop feelings of trust; see Cripwell, 1979:41. For a more detailed account of the use of group preparation in an in-service situation, see Wallace, 1981a.)

6.13 'The teach'

This is the interactive stage of the microteaching programme, where the trainee has to put into practice what she has planned. 'The teach' normally lasts, as has been noted, for five to ten minutes: this is usually all that is necessary to cover the given task or skill. Experience shows that even such a short period of teaching is sufficient to generate useful discussion for at least half an hour and sometimes longer. During 'the teach', the tutor should make a note of points that may prove a useful focus for reflective discussion.

6.14 Peer teaching

An important aspect of 'the teach' concerns the 'students'. Here there are two possibilities. The first is 'peer teaching' (role play) where trainees take the part of students; the other alternative, of course, is to use real students. The original Stanford programme used real students at the appropriate grade or level. There are clearly logistical problems involved in this procedure, and also there is a possible 'cost' factor in terms of disruption of the students' education. But how far is it possible and valid for trainee teachers to take the part of learners? Ward (1970) found that in the United States, in secondary teacher education programmes, trainees were used much more frequently than real students. Stoddart (1981:30) found that of the eleven UK TEFL institutions that he visited only one used learners to form the class and even then only occasionally. Various reasons have been put forward to justify the peer-teaching procedure, for example, that it gives insight into learning problems by putting the teacher in the learner's shoes, so to speak. The involvement of peers in a learning role can also promote lively discussion.

There are various ways of handling the simulation aspect of peer-group role play. It can simply be announced to the participants that they represent a class of learners at level X (whatever that level might be). Geddes and Raz (1979:59–63) have described a more elaborate approach using role-play cards. This was very successful, but with a 'happy well-knit group'. Another way round the unreal aspect of using peers is to make the task *the same in kind* but at a different level. Thus, reading skills may be tackled at a level appropriate to the participants rather than at a lower level.

Having said all that, the conclusion must be that, generally speaking, nothing works so well as using real learners. Only then is the true nature of the teaching and learning process revealed at the appropriate level.

6.15 Recording 'the teach'

There are basically three possibilities for recording 'the teach', which might be labelled as *high-tech*, *low-tech* and *without hardware*. The high-tech approach involves the use of one or more video cameras, either of the portable kind in an ordinary classroom, or standard cameras in a studio. Low-tech involves the use of one or more ordinary audio cassette recorders. I have used this technique in a variety of situations in several different countries, and it has proved remarkably effective in providing a point of reference, especially for those who have been participants in, or observers of, the original 'teach' (Wallace, 1981*a*). The 'microteaching without hardware' approach has been described by Lawless (1971), who used a reporting-back procedure by observers. As the availability of hardware proliferates, however, the undoubted convenience of electronic playback will probably prove increasingly attractive.

Some commentators have expressed reservations about microteaching (especially where video taping is involved) for the pressure it can put on the individual teacher. This aspect undoubtedly has to be handled carefully especially in short courses, where members of the group have not had time to build up intra-group relationships, or in courses involving experienced and more senior teachers. In these circumstances, group preparation of the microlesson undoubtedly helps, as noted in 6.12 above. Care and tact must be shown, and microteaching should never be imposed on a group if they are not ready for it. The procedure should be to allow the group time to settle down and get to know one another before the programme begins, and for the tutor to be sensitive to the mood of the group. This problem is not so acute with younger or undergraduate trainees.

6.16 Analysis and discussion (critique)

The analysis and discussion requires very careful handling on the part of the supervisor. The first question might very well be: Is the supervisor's presence really necessary? There were some early findings that the supervisor's presence was not necessary, indeed counterproductive, but these findings were questioned by McKnight (1971:32). McIntyre (1977:129) conducted some experimentation at Stirling University to see if costs could be lessened by savings in the use of supervisors' time during microteaching critiques. His findings were that the acquisition of skills did not appear to be influenced by the presence or absence of tutors, but that groups working without a tutor suffered from lower morale. He was therefore not able to recommend the use of tutorless critique groups.

Given McIntyre's findings, the most useful function of the supervisor might well be that of harnessing the trainees' own powers of analysis. The 'teacher' of the microlesson should usually be given the first opportunity to comment on the lesson, perhaps by explaining what she was trying to do, and whether or not the lesson went as she had planned it. In such circumstances, the 'teacher' is often overly self-critical, thus giving the tutor and the rest of the group the opportunity to be reassuring and generally supportive.

During the microlesson analysis itself, a most effective technique is often simply to stop the tape from time to time at significant moments and to ask the 'teacher' or the other trainees to comment. If it is clear that the group have not grasped the significance of the episode, then it can be replayed and/or some kind of prompt can be given. The prompt might very well take the form of a question related to prescribed reading or a recent lecture, for example, 'How does what we have just seen fit with X's article on teaching reading / our tutorial discussion yesterday?' As far as possible, trainees must be encouraged to develop their own insights with some kind of reflective and informed basis.

Another way of providing an agenda for discussion is to focus the analysis of microlessons by using skill-specific observation schedules of the kind which were discussed in the previous chapter. Gregory (1972), Wallace (1981b) and Perrott (1982) provide examples of this approach. This issue, and others relating to supervision practice generally, will be taken up in the next chapter.

6.17 'The reteach'

In the original 'applied science' model of microteaching, 'the reteach' was an essential part of the microteaching process. The criterion for becoming a competent teacher (or, at least, of moving on to the next stage of professional development) was to demonstrate the possession of certain identified 'skills'. Obviously, if these skills were not mastered at the first attempt, they would have to be attempted again (by means of a reteach or perhaps several reteaches) until competence was demonstrated. In practice, very few institutions can afford the luxury of repeated attempts at a given skill, so, where reteaches are organised, it is usually on the basis of one for each skill.

A corollary of this model is that *all* the trainees must attempt *all* the skills: this again for most institutions would assume either a limited number of trainees and/or a tightly-controlled number of skills.

When should 'the reteach' take place? One possibility is that it should take place almost immediately, while the critique is still fresh in the trainee's mind. It is the experience of many teacher educators that such an arrangement is too rushed: for example, at Stirling University, after a good deal of experimentation, the period between 'teach' and 'reteach' was expanded to a week. As against this, my colleague, Patricia Ahrens, has devised a simple and flexible technique using *pairs* of trainees, where both are jointly responsible but one does 'the teach' and the other 'the reteach'. The experience of tutors using this approach is that it works well and that perceptible progress can be achieved even if only thirty minutes is allowed for the preparation of 'the reteach'.

As I have said before, the reflective approach to microteaching is based on quite different assumptions about professional education from the applied science approach. Professional competence is not a matter of mastering a range of skills which, for purely practical reasons, must remain fairly narrow. Indeed, the reflective model raises the question as to whether 'skills' interpreted in a strict sense are central or peripheral to professional development. Rather, the reflective approach regards microteaching episodes as opportunities for experiential learning with respect to conceptual, and perhaps also affective, development. This learning experience may be of two kinds: either *personal*, in the direct experience of attempting the microteaching task as a 'teacher', or *vicarious*, in the sense of being an observer of such teaching or perhaps being the recipient of such teaching as a 'learner' in a peer-group teaching situation.

One implication of the reflective approach might be that, far from restricting the range of microteaching tasks, it might be as well to go for the greatest variety of such tasks that is possible within the resource allocation for any given training course. The different tasks might afford a richer context for the discussion of key concepts of the course, like, for example:

the correction of error,
the nature and effect of various questioning techniques,
the promotion of student participation,
the development of motivation,
clarity of exposition,
the management of feedback,
utilisation of student input in, for example, composition,
promotion of more realistic use of language for communication, and
    so on.

Similarly, it is not necessary, or perhaps even desirable, for every trainee to attempt every task. Reflection-in-action is a necessary aspect of professional learning, but reflection-on-action by observation can be a useful complement to it.

Where does all this leave someone attempting to plan a microteaching programme?

First, it must be recognised that there are good reasons for having a 'reteach' facility apart from the behavioural rationale put forward by the original proponents of microteaching. There may be certain techniques or skills which the programme designer deems to be essential for her trainees. Trainees who have done a bad microlesson may wish to attempt it again to regain their confidence. The programme designers may therefore, if resources permit, wish to build in the opportunity for a certain amount of 'remedial' microteaching. However, if the point of view just presented is accepted, it is not absolutely necessary for all trainees to practise all the skills or tasks, nor for *every* skill or task to be repeated according to the 'reteach' format. At the same time, the formal marking of 'progress', which is one of the strengths of the original model, should be preserved if at all possible. In this respect, it is important that the reflection and discussion on the various microlesson tasks should be articulated in a summary or review form: this might be in the form of a summary of the main issues and conclusions on the blackboard, or in the form of a handout, based on notes taken during the discussion, distributed at the beginning of the next session. As I have said, skill-specific or task-specific observation schedules can also play an important role in helping trainees to articulate and objectify their reflection on the skill or task in question. Such data, whether it takes the form of notes, handouts, schedules, or whatever, should be kept in the trainees' 'teaching experience file' for future reference and review as necessary.

6.18 Microteaching and assessment

Should microteaching be used for assessment purposes? In many microteaching programmes it is. Describing the education programme at the New University of Ulster, McGarvey and Swallow (1986:26) note that the assessment of trainees is based on 70% for the practical work (including microteaching with 'real' learners) and 30% for the written examination. They go on to note that: 'This is a major influence on students' [trainees'] approaches to their microteaching and to their relationships with their tutor. Tutors too find assessment a major influence on their work.'

It is clear, from what McGarvey and Swallow say, that the assessment of microteaching is something which has to be considered very carefully, since it significantly changes the nature of the process both for the tutor and for the trainee. One problem, as they go on to point out, is that tutors have to try to combine the roles of adviser and examiner. This combination of formative and evaluative roles is always problematic, and is probably best avoided if at all possible. It certainly makes the use of collaborative supervision (described in the next chapter) much more difficult.

A second argument against using microteaching for assessment is the artificial nature of the technique. Of course, it is true to say that *all* training situations (including teaching practice) are 'artificial' to some extent. However, there are degrees of artificiality, and microteaching is usually a good bit further along the cline of artificiality than teaching practice. This is not to say that it should *never* be used directly with assessment: in the case of the New University of Ulster, it seems to be used partly as a selection device to sort out potentially effective teachers from those who might be best suited to a more academic, non-teaching path.

It is also possible for microteaching to be linked *indirectly* to assessment. Cousin and others (1978) have described a pre-service TEFL programme for Saudi Arabian teachers being trained in the UK (at Moray House College). In that programme, the trainees were assessed *not* on their microteaching performance (peer-group teaching), but on the demonstration of their ability *to reflect critically on* and *to self-evaluate* their own teaching. This was done in the form of an oral examination, in which a tape of their own teaching was played back for the trainees, and they made whatever comments they thought appropriate on it in discussion with their tutor and another assessor.

On the whole, it seems more productive, in formative terms, to avoid linking assessment to microteaching directly, although it could be a useful tool for assessing the trainees' powers of self-evaluation.

6.19 Extended microteaching

If you look back to Figures 6.1 and 6.2 you will be reminded that microteaching is one of a cline of experiential learning activities. In this sense, extended forms of microteaching form a kind of bridge onto the next stage of 'supervised professional action'. As Stoddart has noted (1981:57–60), extended microteaching can take two forms, which we shall call *linked microlessons* and *minilessons*.

1. **Linked microlessons**   These are a form of team teaching in which a group of trainees is responsible for different stages of a lesson. This can be done *either* by the trainees preparing the lesson together as a whole, and then deciding who does which part, *or* by each trainee being assigned an activity in a sequence of activities which have a

common topic or common content. The former would seem preferable and seems to be more common (Stoddart, 1981:59).

2. **Minilessons** These are simply longer microlessons (perhaps twenty minutes), which may tend to have a more diffuse focus but which may also approximate more closely to a 'real' lesson. It is possible, of course, for there to be a specific focus even in a longer lesson.

Summary

Microteaching is now a well established and highly valued teacher education technique. This is perhaps because it occupies a key place in the cline of activities which allow for safe experimentation as a means of developing professional action. Microteaching traditionally has four stages: the briefing, 'the teach', the critique (analysis and discussion), and 'the reteach'. Microteaching, however, is also a very flexible technique, and each of these stages allows for a wide range of variation in implementation. How microteaching is implemented will, to some extent, depend on whether the underlying philosophy relates to the 'applied science' approach or the 'reflective' approach. It will also depend on other factors, such as what is understood by the term 'skill', as well as various administrative and resource constraints.

Various forms of extended microteaching also exist, notably 'linked microlessons', and the longer 'minilessons'.

PERSONAL REVIEW

See if you can form a 'self-help' group with four or five other trainers. Draw up a list of teaching tasks using material that is *appropriate to the level of the group* (i.e. adult tasks). Select some of the tasks and teach them to the other members of the group. Each microlesson should not last more than five to ten minutes and should be audio taped. Play it back and analyse or discuss it in the group. Keep notes of problems that you encounter (e.g. sensitivity to criticism, problems of 'unreality' of the process, difficulty of separating out performance skills, etc.). At the end of each session make a brief summary of what, if anything, you have learned about: (a) the performance skills of teaching, and (b) the 'critique' (analysis and discussion) stage of microteaching.

---

7 Supervision and practical experience

7.1 Overview

In this chapter, I will pay special attention to the topic of supervision, and in particular, 'clinical supervision'. I will draw a distinction between 'general supervision' and 'clinical supervision'. 'General supervision' is more concerned with administrative and 'out of classroom' matters, while 'clinical supervision' is more concerned with formative (training) aspects of classroom teaching.

Various ways of categorising 'clinical supervision' will be looked at, but I will suggest that a simple division could be made between a more *prescriptive* approach and a more *collaborative* approach. I will discuss some of the implications of adopting a more collaborative approach, and there is a short description of some ways in which practical experience might be organised. Again, the chapter concludes with a substantial 'Personal review' section.

7.2 Supervisors and supervision

The discussion of supervision can be quite confusing because of the wide variety of terms used to describe those engaged in supervision, and the wide range of definitions of the term itself. In this chapter, the word *supervisor* will be used in a very broad sense to cover a variety of other terms which you might prefer to use in your own situation. A supervisor, in this sense, is anyone who has, as a substantial element in her or his professional remit, the duty of monitoring and improving the quality of teaching done by other colleagues in a given educational situation. Among the people who might have such a function are: inspectors, teacher trainers, educators, tutors, advisers, counsellors, heads of departments, head-teachers, consultants, field supervisors, curriculum specialists, regents, supervisory teachers, 'conseillers/animateurs pedagogiques', and, of course (but all too seldom), classroom teachers themselves. For all those mentioned, and any others who have not been mentioned, we can use the term *supervisor* when they are engaged in this particular function. In the present context, the particular focus is on teacher trainers as supervisors, whether for pre-service or in-service courses.

7.3 General and clinical supervision

A useful distinction has been drawn between *general supervision* and *clinical supervision* (see, for example, Cogan, 1973; Sergiovanni and Starratt, 1983:291). General supervision refers to what might be called the 'administrative' aspects of supervision or 'out of class' supervision. It is therefore concerned with such issues as curriculum, syllabus and the overall management structure of education both outside and within the school. Clinical supervision, on the other hand, is concerned with what goes on inside the classroom: in the words of Sergiovanni and Starratt (1983:292) it 'refers to contact with teachers with the intent of improving instruction and increasing growth', and they quote Goldhammer's phrase that clinical supervision implies 'supervision up close' (Goldhammer, 1969:54). Sergiovanni and Starratt rightly point out that, of course, the two areas of supervision are interdependent. However, the consideration of such issues as curriculum, syllabus and educational management and administration would take us well beyond the scope of the present discussion. In this chapter, I will therefore be concerned almost exclusively with the issue of clinical supervision in the broad sense that has just been given.

7.4 Clinical supervision

It is unfortunate that the term *clinical supervision* shares with all too many neologisms in language methodology and education generally the qualities of being simultaneously opaque and somewhat misleading.

Smyth (1986:1–2) acknowledges this problem and explains how the term 'clinical supervision' was coined by Morris Cogan and his associates because they were concerned to find a way in which 'theory could emerge out of practice, rather than exclusively being "applied" to practice as is so often the case'. This quotation, however, exemplifies another problem with the way the term is used. 'Clinical supervision' is often used not only to describe a certain mode of professional learning (i.e. face-to-face and classroom-centred), but also to imply a certain attitude *as to how that mode ought to be conducted*. In the terms which have been used in this book, it implies a rejection of the 'applied science' model and an acceptance of the 'reflective' model of professional development. There is thus a potential for confusion here: are we talking about a training mode or about a method of implementing it? The problem is compounded by the fact that even within the tradition of

Cogan's approach, 'numerous disagreements over concepts and methods . . . exist among various advocates of the model' (Zeichner and Liston, 1985:157). The full extent of disagreement over how clinical supervision is to be implemented has been very clearly described by Retallick (1986), ranging as it does from a very prescriptive approach at one end to a very egalitarian approach at the other.

There seem to be good grounds for agreeing with Smyth that the term 'clinical supervision' is now too well established to be dispensed with. However, it is argued here that, in the interests of clarity, 'clinical supervision' should be reserved for a particular mode of training, namely face-to-face interaction between a supervisor and a teacher, or group of teachers, with reference to some classroom teaching that has previously been observed, the aim of the interaction being to discuss and analyse the teaching with a view to professional development of the teacher or teachers concerned.

Varieties of clinical supervision

Having established a working definition of 'clinical supervision' as a training mode, we can now turn to the problem raised in the previous section: the fact that it can be implemented in a variety of ways.

In an interesting article, Freeman (1982) notes three approaches to observing in-service teachers: these he calls: (1) the *supervisory approach*, with the observer as authority and arbitrator; (2) the *alternatives approach*, with the observer as a provider of 'alternative perspectives'; and (3) the *non-directive approach*, with the observer as 'understander'. In a subsequent article, Gebhard (1984) presents a stimulating overview of supervision in which he increases the number of possible models to five, as follows: (1) *directive supervision*, in which the supervisor's role is to direct and inform good model teaching and finally evaluate; (2) *alternative supervision*, in which alternatives may be suggested either by the supervisor (as with Freeman), or by the trainee; (3) *collaborative supervision*, in which the supervisor 'actively participates with the teacher in any decisions that are made and attempts to establish a sharing relationship' (*ibid.*:505); (4) *non-directive supervision*, in which the supervisor is similarly non-judgemental as in (3), but does not *share* responsibility: that resides with the trainee, to whom the supervisor simply provides an 'understanding response' in Curran's (1978) phrase; and finally (5) *creative supervision*, in which the supervisor uses any combination of the above, or shifts the responsibility to another source (e.g. another teacher), or uses insights from other fields.

The above accounts of Freeman's and Gebhard's articles are necessarily compressed and omit much anecdotal and exemplificatory material that is of interest to the language teacher educator. Reading them (and especially Gebhard's article), it seems possible that, like many other human processes, supervision is capable of almost infinite division. This is reinforced by other attempts to categorise supervision: Retallick's (1986) three-field division, for example, is different from either of those referred to although it overlaps with them in various ways.

Perhaps one way to categorise clinical supervision usefully yet simply is to view it as a series of possible supervisory behaviours in which a tendency to one of two approaches will probably be detectable: we could call these the *prescriptive approach* and the *collaborative approach*. The 'classic' position of these approaches might be contrasted as in Figure 7.1. Some supervisors may show characteristics of both approaches in the same supervisory conference, or may use more of one approach with less experienced student teachers and more of the other approach with qualified and experienced teachers.

Classic prescriptive approach	**Classic collaborative approach**
1. Supervisor as authority figure	1. Supervisor as colleague
2. Supervisor as only source of expertise	2. Supervisor and trainee or teacher as co-sharers of expertise
3. Supervisor judges	3. Supervisor understands
4. Supervisor applies a 'blueprint' of how lesson ought to be taught	4. Supervisor has no blueprint: accepts lesson in terms of what trainee or teacher is attempting to do
5. Supervisor talks; trainee listens	5. Supervisor considers listening as important as talking
6. Supervisor attempts to preserve authority and mystique	6. Supervisor attempts to help trainee or teacher develop autonomy, through practice in reflection and self-evaluation

Figure 7.1   Approaches to clinical supervision (after Sergiovanni, 1977)

Prescriptive and collaborative approaches

Looking at Figure 7.1 we see that in the *prescriptive approach*, in its 'classic' form, the supervisor is seen as an authority figure. The supervisor has 'expert' status, knows what ought to be done in a given teaching situation and is in a position to tell the trainee what she has done wrong and what she can do to put it right. In the *collaborative approach*, on the other hand, the supervisor and the trainee are seen as colleagues, with perhaps different functions and responsibilities. Each acknowledges the other's different expertise: perhaps the trainee is more familiar with the class and the school context; perhaps the supervisor has much more experience in seeing a variety of approaches to teaching. The supervisor reacts to the lesson in the light of what she thinks the trainee is attempting to achieve. A main aim is to allow the trainee to express her own reflections and self-evaluation so that she can pursue her own professional development more effectively.

The prescriptive approach

Many of the educationalists who have written about clinical supervision have firmly repudiated what has been called here the 'prescriptive approach'. Indeed, for some, the very term 'clinical supervision' is synonymous with the rejection of such an approach to supervision. Very often this rejection is ideological. In discussing the 'prescriptive approach' (but not using that label) Smyth (1986:60) says: 'It is not the teachers' agendas, issues and concerns that are being addressed, but rather those of someone within the administrative or bureaucratic hierarchy. What really is at issue is the question of who exercises power.'

It is interesting to observe that the language specialists who have written about the prescriptive approach to clinical supervision (under whatever name they have given it) have tended to be much more tolerant of it, and have even seen a place for it. Freeman, for example, sees a place for this approach at Stage I in his 'hierarchy of needs': 'In fact, there can be a certain security for both people [i.e. the supervisor and the trainee] in knowing what is expected and in regarding performance in those terms' (Freeman, 1982:22). Gebhard is much more critical of the shortcomings of very prescriptive supervision, of which he gives a rather horrific example from his own personal experience. However, he does make reference to Copeland's (1982) research which showed that: 'Some teachers feel the need to be told what to do when they first begin to teach. He [Copeland] attributes this to their insecurity in facing students without having the skills to cope with that situation. Teachers from a number of countries have pointed out that if the teacher is not given direction by the supervisor, then the supervisor is not considered qualified. The roots of directive supervision grow deep' (Gebhard, 1984:504). Similarly, Bowers (1987:138) sees a need for both training, which is more prescriptive, and counselling, which is more collaborative: 'A programme of training is essentially process-oriented: it is a means of developing in a cohort of teachers, normally within a group context, a set of desired skills or habits, frequently relating to a given curriculum or set of materials. It is prospective, directed towards prescribed ends. Counselling, by contrast, is person-oriented . . .'

PERSONAL REVIEW

Look again at Figure 7.1. See if you can clarify your own thinking about the six elements that have been listed there with respect to clinical supervision in any situation you are familiar with, by circling the appropriate number (1–7) in the grid below.

So, in the first element, if you think that, in the situation you are considering, a supervisor ought to function simply as another colleague and not at all as an authority figure, then you will circle 7; if you think that the supervisor ought to have equal qualities of 'authority figure' and 'colleague' then you will mark 4; and so on. Note that, whenever you choose one of the middle range figures, you must ask yourself how far it is actually *possible* to combine the two approaches at the same time. Compare your figures with other colleagues.

Element	Prescriptive						Collaborative
1. Authority	1	2	3	4	5	6	7
2. Expertise	1	2	3	4	5	6	7
3. Judgement / Understanding	1	2	3	4	5	6	7
4. Blueprint	1	2	3	4	5	6	7
5. Talking / Listening	1	2	3	4	5	6	7
6. Mystique / Autonomy	1	2	3	4	5	6	7

7.5 Supervision styles in microteaching

At this stage it might be useful to look at a categorisation of supervision styles which is based on field research data. Reference has already been made to the work of McGarvey and Swallow (1986) with reference to microteaching (in Chapter 6). An important part of that study was a systematic analysis of the supervisory styles adopted by the microteaching tutors at the New University of Ulster. In the study, the authors detect two approaches to microteaching supervision. Both approaches are discussed in the context of a general education pre-service training programme. They label the first 'Practice for Classroom Teaching' (PCT) approach. PCT approach tutors opted for a 'direct' (i.e. overtly prescriptive) supervisory strategy, because of the inexperience of the trainees. They were concerned, among other things, with discussing shortcomings in the lesson and with making suggestions for improvement. The second is labelled the 'Teaching Concept Development' (TCD) approach. Tutors using this strategy claimed to adopt an 'indirect' (i.e. non-prescriptive or not overtly prescriptive) strategy, and claimed to be concerned about 'supportive interpersonal relations' (McGarvey and Swallow, 1986:78). It will be seen that these two approaches roughly correspond to what Bowers (1987) has called the 'training' and 'counselling' approaches to supervision. An added dimension is revealed by the labels which McGarvey and Swallow give to the two approaches: namely that the 'Practice for Classroom Teaching' (PCT) approach is more short term and closely focussed on immediate classroom teaching issues, whereas the 'Teaching Concept Development' (TCD) approach is less concerned with seeking remedies for immediate difficulties, and more concerned with helping trainees to build their own conceptual framework of teaching. It should perhaps be emphasised that, although analysis of the taped supervision conferences with the trainees showed that the approaches of the PCT and TCD tutors were 'clearly distinguishable' (*ibid*.:90), this is in *statistical terms*. In other words, the supervisory behaviour of the two approaches overlapped in many ways, but to a different degree. For example, both groups of tutors used questions to promote student analysis, but TCD tutors devoted about three-quarters of their questions to promoting student analysis, while PCT tutors employed only about one quarter of their questions for this purpose (*ibid*.:90).

Effect of different supervisory styles in microteaching

What were the effects of the two contrasting supervisory styles which McGarvey and Swallow discovered? The first interesting finding was that the students revealed an awareness of the supervisors' approaches and responded differently to them. In other words, students who were taught by PCT tutors tended as a group to hold certain views about their relationships with their tutors, and those who were taught by TCD tutors had different views, as a group. What were the different reactions of the students? The PCT (directive/prescriptive) approach was acknowledged to have certain advantages, but, on the other hand: 'Without exception, the students did not find this a valuable way to proceed. They claimed to know themselves what problems they were having, and described the approach that their tutors favoured as being rigid and uncompromising. More seriously perhaps, this promoted a feeling that the tutor was distant and unapproachable. Students wanted to talk about their concerns but felt that the atmosphere did not allow it' (*ibid*.:129). Within the TCD (non-directive, more collaborative) approach, on the other hand, the students 'regarded their tutors highly for their flexibility and sensitivity toward them as individuals . . . The students did not consider the tutors' persistent quests for analysis to be threatening; rather they appreciated that this was a valuable means of probing the complexities of teaching.'

In terms of student reactions, therefore, the weight of opinion comes down clearly against what we have called the more prescriptive approach, and in favour of what has been called here the more 'collaborative' approach. But it should be noted again that the PCT ('prescriptive') approach also had positive effects, for example, in terms of confidence in planning and presentation, experience with classroom aids, etc. (*ibid.*:131).

Effects of different supervisory styles on in-service teachers

The subjects in the research done by McGarvey and Swallow were all pre-service trainees. What are the reactions of experienced, in-service teachers to different supervisory styles? We have already noted Gebhard's evidence concerning positive teacher reactions to a prescriptive supervisory approach, particularly with reference to Copeland's (1982) research (see page 111).

Further evidence on this issue is provided by Perlberg and Theodor (1975:208), who analysed the reactions of a group of twenty teachers of culturally disadvantaged elementary school pupils to the supervisory styles of five supervisors. All twenty teachers had between five and fifteen years' experience of teaching. Their findings for our present concerns may be summarised by this extract (italics not in original):

> '*The patterns most preferred by the teachers* were task orientation and relevance to the lessons, relevant encouragement and positive rewards, talking in a pleasant tone, understanding the teacher, allowing the teacher to express herself, clarity, simplicity, and polite criticism accompanied by practical advice. *The most rejected patterns* were sharp or exclusive criticism, aggressiveness, "cross-examination", lack of positive rewards, imposing of opinions and knowing everything better than the teacher, not permitting the teacher to talk, rejection of teacher's action and speech, lengthy monologues, dwelling on general or marginal issues, confusion and lack of practical advice . . . [The teachers] expected the supervisor to know what was right and what was wrong and to tell them what to do and how to do it. All they requested was that it be done in a kind and pleasant manner . . . No teacher complained about the obvious absence of encouraging intellectual autonomy, independent inquiry, analysis, planning and self-evaluation.'

Implications for the conduct of supervision

Where does all this leave the supervisor? McGarvey and Swallow's findings seem to indicate that the more prescriptive PCT approach was badly evaluated by the trainee teachers as opposed to the more collaborative TCD approach; whereas Perlberg and Theodor seem to indicate that teachers welcome 'pleasant authoritarianism' (*ibid.*:208).

We can begin by looking more closely at the traits which characterise the most preferred supervisor in Perlberg and Theodor's study:

> 'She speaks in a pleasant tone, encourages the teacher, refers to the essentials of the lesson and explains her opinions clearly and in order. She starts from the positive features and builds on them. She does not ignore the negative aspects of the lesson, but she expresses her opinion in a kind manner, so that it is easy to accept. She makes suggestions and gives practical advice without trying to impose her opinion. She allows the teacher to express herself and understands her.'

When we analyse this description, we see that the overall strategy is clearly 'prescriptive' but that it also contains some elements which would fit quite well under the 'collaborative' heading, for example, the supervisor does not try 'to impose her opinion'; she 'allows the teacher to express herself'; she 'understands her'. There are also features which are strictly speaking neutral such as speaking 'in a pleasant tone'; she is 'clear'; she is organised in the way she explains things; she is 'kind' even while criticising. Such features, however, or some of them, might also indicate a mutual professional respect which might not so readily occur in someone anxious to preserve her authority.

It is interesting that the McGarvey and Swallow data show the way in which a more prescriptive or more collaborative approach can change the affective dimension of the interaction. It might be reasonable to assume that the more prescriptive PCT tutors were no more or less pleasant as people, on average, than the TCD tutors. Yet because the PCT tutors saw it as their role and their duty to discriminate between their trainees' strengths and weaknesses, the effect on the trainees was to make the supervisors seem 'distant and unapproachable', as has been noted earlier. McGarvey and Swallow highlight the importance of the 'affective learning dimension' in this view, and see the TCD (collaborative) style as a formative element in promoting the appropriate kind of affective learning, initially for the trainees, but ultimately also for the benefit of the trainees' students: 'The competent teacher is not only a good teacher but also a good learner' (*ibid.*:160).

Supervisory approaches and reflective practice

There is another aspect of the Perlberg and Theodor findings which ought to be discussed. This is the apparent lack of interest shown by their teacher subjects in 'intellectual autonomy, independent inquiry, analysis, planning and self-evaluation'.

There are two points that can be made about this. The first point is that, unlike the trainees in McGarvey and Swallow's research, those teachers did not get the chance to compare the more 'collaborative' Teacher Concept Development type of supervisor with the more 'prescriptive' Practice for Classroom Teaching type of supervisor. The supervisors were all of the latter type. We therefore do not know how they would have reacted to a more collaborative approach had they been given the opportunity.

The second point is that if the concept of 'reflective practice' as it has been presented here has any validity at all, the fostering of 'intellectual autonomy, independent inquiry, analysis and self-evaluation' must be a desirable goal, even if there is no overt demand in the first instance. The findings of McGarvey and Swallow show that, at least in one context, the pursuit of a deeper type of professional development can be achieved while achieving a considerable degree of consumer satisfaction.

7.6 Supervisory approaches: Conclusions

We can summarise the discussion so far as follows:

1. There are two basic approaches to clinical supervision: one is more 'prescriptive', the other more 'collaborative'.
2. Prescription has its place and its function. Trainees welcome the authority of experience; it gives them confidence and relieves their anxiety.
3. Prescription should always be tempered by mutual respect, a warm and pleasant manner, a lucid and organised presentation of one's point of view, and a recognition of strengths as well as weaknesses. But excessive flattery and not criticising when it is called for are perceived as ineffectiveness (Perlberg and Theodor, 1975:209); and rightly so, since they offend the principle of mutual professional respect.
4. The goal, however, should be increased collaboration: if handled properly, a more collaborative approach is likely to improve the affective relationship between supervisor and trainee; also, through such an approach, the supervisor can hope to foster the conditions for reflective practice and the longer-term professional development of the trainee.

PERSONAL REVIEW

Do you agree that the goal of supervision should be increased collaboration between supervisor and supervisee? If such collaboration were desirable, what forms could it take?

7.7 Implementing collaboration

How is a more collaborative approach to be implemented? A full answer to this question would operate at several levels, but we only have space here to look at two aspects of this problem: (a) the organisation of the clinical supervision process, and (b) the way in which the supervisory process is handled.

Cogan's eight-phase cycle

A truly collaborative approach to supervision is a demanding and time-consuming process. According to Cogan (1973), there should be eight phases in the cycle of supervision:

1. Phase 1 – Teacher and supervisor establish a relationship of mutual trust and support.
2. Phase 2 – Teacher and supervisor plan the lesson, or the series of lessons together.
3. Phase 3 – Teacher and supervisor agree on what and how much will be observed.
4. Phase 4 – The observation.
5. Phase 5 – Teacher and supervisor analyse the events of the lesson, either together, or separately first and then together.
6. Phase 6 – Teacher and supervisor plan how, when and where the supervisory conference will be conducted.
7. Phase 7 – The supervisory conference.
8. Phase 8 – Resumption of planning (cycle begins again – see Phase 2).

Cogan is obviously thinking of a context where a much closer relationship can exist between the supervisor and the teacher than is possible in most situations. Supervision of professional action in a school is already recognised as being a very expensive form of training: it has a training ratio of one-to-one, and it also usually involves travelling time. Cogan's eight-phase cycle would make it even more expensive in those terms. However, there are other possible administrative solutions. In Sri Lanka, for example, there has been some trialling of the use of *field supervisors*: these are practising teachers who are given some time off their normal duties to supervise a small group of trainees over a period of time. Such a system might make Cogan's recommended procedure more economically feasible.

The 'normal' pattern of supervision is, one suspects, much more basic, as follows:

Phase 1 – The observation (Cogan's Phase 4).
Phase 2 – The supervisory conference.

You will have noted that collaboration pervades the pattern of supervision proposed by Cogan: before, after and during the supervision. If this pattern strikes you as simply not being feasible in your own situation for administrative or economic reasons, and if, on the other hand, the basic pattern seems inadequate, then the question might well be asked: which of Cogan's stages are more dispensable?

Various answers are possible. It might be, for example, that the supervisor is also a tutor to the trainee, in which case there has been an opportunity for Phase 1 to be established in class time or during the microteaching programme, etc. Phase 2 may also have at least partially occurred prior to the school experience period; or it might be partially achieved by the trainee preparing the lesson herself and discussing and having it approved by the tutor some time before it has to be taught. Phase 3 might, if necessary, be compressed into a brief pre-lesson discussion, where the trainee might express any anxieties or uncertainties about what she has planned. Phase 6 (details of conference) might be dealt with at the same time. Phase 5 (analysis of events) might be combined with Phase 7 (the conference). It must be stressed that these are not recommendations: they are merely indications of ways in which some of the effects of Cogan's organisation of collaboration might be achieved more economically, albeit probably less effectively. In human relations, there is really no substitute for time.

7.8 Requirements for a reflective dialogue

Before proceeding further with details of the implementation of clinical supervision, perhaps we ought to pause at this point and ask ourselves this question: what are the *essential requirements* for establishing a proper reflective dialogue?

In investigating how knowledge of practice is acquired in the various professions he had selected for study, Schön (1983) discovered four *constants* which the various practitioners brought to their 'reflection-in-action'. The first of these is the range of 'media, languages and repertoires' which practitioners use, and which has previously been discussed in section 6.2 above. The remaining three constants are of relevance here. They are:

1. **Overarching theories** – by which the tutor and the trainee make
    sense of phenomena. It is essential that the tutor and the trainee
    have shared understandings of what teaching in general, and
    language teaching in particular, is all about. This does not
    necessarily mean that they believe in the same theories, although in
    pre-service training this will usually be the case since the trainee has
    not had time to develop her own. If the supervisor and the trainee

can both agree on what the process and the product of the lesson ought to be, this is a big step forward. A common problem arises, however, when a trainee has given intellectual assent to one theory (*espoused theory*), but actually teaches according to another (*theory in use*). (These terms are discussed in Sergiovanni and Starratt, 1983:306.) It might be, for example, that a trainee claims to be teaching a 'communicative' lesson which strikes the observer as not being communicative at all. This is an issue which obviously has to be explored with the trainee.

2. **Appreciative (or value) systems** – which the supervisor and trainee bring to the reflective dialogue. By this, one understands Schön to mean the values shared by both participants: what is important and what is not, what is 'successful' and what is not, and so on. It is always an interesting exercise to show a group of experienced teachers someone else's lesson on video tape and, in an open-ended, free-wheeling way, ask them to comment on what they have seen. There is almost always a wide range of value judgements about the effectiveness of the lesson, or parts of the lesson, to say nothing of what aspects some think worth commenting on which others ignore or take for granted. If this is true of experienced teachers, it is even more important with a teacher in training for the supervisor to discover 'where the trainee is at' in terms of her powers of establishing mature and thoughtful value systems.

3. **Role frames** The role frame is crucial for understanding the reflective dialogue between the supervisor and the trainee. How does the supervisor see herself and her function? Does she see it as her job to advise and correct the trainee according to some predetermined principles? Does she see her role as capable of evolving and changing or is it fixed, perhaps, within some bureaucratic framework? And what of the trainee? Does she regard herself as an empty, ignorant vessel that the supervisor will hopefully fill with expertise? Or is the whole thing a meaningless charade, or perhaps a game that you can win if you somehow guess what the hidden rules are? Perhaps the 'rules of the game' ought to be made clear and explicit.

Need for focus

To these constants which Schön has postulated, one might wish to add another: the need for *focus* in the supervisory conference. It has been noted several times in this book what a complex, multi-faceted activity teaching is. The amount of data generated by even a section of a lesson is almost overwhelming when subjected to close reflective analysis. Somehow, this welter of data has to be focussed, limited and filtered so that it can be effectively handled.

With these general issues in mind, let us return once more to the problem of the organisation of clinical supervision.

7.9 Bowers' teacher counselling guide

A six-phase pattern for clinical supervision has been suggested by Bowers (1987), to which he has given the mnemonic acronym HORACE, standing for: Hear – Observe – Record – Analyse – Consider – Evaluate. It will be worth our while to look at this pattern more closely, especially as it has been presented within the context of a foreign language teaching situation: specifically, the teacher education pro-grammes at the Centre for the Development of English Language Teaching (CDELT), at Ain Shams University, Cairo.

1. and 2. **Hear and Observe**   Bowers points out that it is not enough to observe a teacher's performance. You must first place it in the context of the trainee's understanding, and be aware of what she thinks important or unimportant, and so on. It will be clear that these concerns relate closely to the issues raised by Schön's professional 'constants'. Thus, the importance of *hearing* or listening to the teacher. Do her theories or values match the supervisor's? If they don't, it is probably advisable for the supervisor to wait and see the follow-through in the form of the lesson, rather than do anything at this stage which might undermine the teacher's self-confidence. Perhaps the performance itself will be a useful context for the discussion of issues of principle.

   Observation should be just that, with no interference at all, if that is possible, with the lesson.

3. and 4. **Record and Analyse**   We noted earlier the need for focus in observation, and in Chapter 6 we discussed a wide, but necessarily incomplete range of ways in which data can be recorded and analysed. Sometimes the focus will be provided by an assessment schedule, as described in the next chapter.

   I have suggested elsewhere (Wallace, 1988) that a simple solution would be a list of questions possibly agreed between the trainee and the supervisor, or possibly used as a formula, for example:

   i)   *The facts:*   What happened? This allows the teacher to give her version of the lesson.

   ii) *Objectives and achievements:*   What were the objectives? What did the students learn?

   iii) *Alternatives:*   Was there *anything else* (not necessarily better) that could have been done? (This often causes problems, and may be omitted, certainly at the early stages.)

iv) *Self-evaluation* What have you (the teacher) learned? (It would obviously be a good thing for the supervisor also to reflect on what she has learned at the end – but that may be a different story!)

5. and 6. **Consider and Evaluate** Bowers rightly advises against a 'rush to judgement'! It is probably better to ask more questions, and get as much of the evaluation as possible done by the teacher herself.

7.10 Organisation and management of practical experience

Finally, this chapter will conclude with a very brief discussion of the organisation and management of practical experience. Controlled and carefully-staged practical experience is, of course, an essential part of any professional training programme. It is also usually the most time-consuming and (therefore) expensive part of such programmes.

We might begin by distinguishing four commonly-used terms: teaching practice, professional action, school experience and placement. *Teaching practice* refers to the opportunity given to the trainee to develop and improve her professional practice in the context of a real classroom, usually under some form of guidance or supervision. *Professional action* is the term used to refer to normal teaching and thus does not have the same connotation of learner status: it is therefore sometimes considered a more convenient term to use, since it can cover in-service as well as pre-service training. By *school experience* we mean the total experience of working in a school which trainees have when they are *on placement*, i.e. when they have been allocated to a particular school as part of their professional development. It is a wider term then than *teaching practice*, which refers to only one aspect of school experience. Apart from teaching, there are many other things which trainees should learn about schools, not only theoretically but also experientially: these include such issues as school management, disciplinary procedures, staff relations, appropriate professional behaviour both inside and outside the classroom, and so on.

In many training schemes, for language teachers (e.g. some of the Royal Society of Arts / UCLES programmes – see end of chapter) the emphasis is very much on teaching practice / professional action, and this is the case especially when the training is done in the same institution where much of the teaching practice is done. In other programmes, the emphasis is mainly on teaching practice within the context of school experience.

Staging of practical experience

On pre-service courses of the B.Ed. type, three ways of staging practical experience can be distinguished (the term 'school experience' will be used, since this is the term most commonly used on such courses):

1. **Serial school experience**   In this arrangement, the school experience runs parallel with, and is usually closely integrated with, college training. Serial school experience is usually organised on a basis of one or two days per week, with perhaps an occasional half-day. Generally, the first school experience in a course will be arranged on a serial basis.

2. **Block school experience**   In this, the trainee spends an uninterrupted block of time in a school: perhaps five weeks, or even a whole term. There may, of course, be an occasional half-day or so back in college for pooling of and reflection on the experience.

3. **Internship**   This is a kind of block school experience which takes place at the end of the college course. Thus, a trainee might spend the first two years of training based in college, probably with opportunities for serial and block school experience. The final year might take the form of an internship, where the teacher is not yet fully qualified, and is still under college supervision, but will have no more formal classes. Interns should be distinguished from *probationers*, who are trainees who have graduated as teachers from college, and no longer have formal links with it, but who are not yet fully confirmed as qualified professionals. (It should be noted that 'intern' is used in some situations to describe any trainee teacher.)

Liaison with schools

Liaison between the training institute and the school is clearly of crucial importance. Sometimes the relationship is purely formal and administrative, and communication is solely with the school principal or the head of department. This has very often proved to be unsatisfactory, since there may be no machinery to ensure that the training objectives of the college and the school coincide, or even that the school sees itself as a partner in the training process.

It is therefore becoming more common for certain members of the school staff to have a specific training function. One of the more elaborate of such schemes has been described by McIntyre (1988) in his account of the innovative teacher education scheme run by the University of Oxford Department of Educational Studies (OUDES). In this scheme, one experienced teacher called a *Mentor* coordinates the classroom-related experiences of each trainee throughout the year.

There is also the *Professional tutor* who has the job of coordinating all the trainees' programmes in the school. (In Scotland, the person holding such a post is called a *Regent*.) There are also members of OUDES staff who are attached to the school with other coordinating and liaison functions. (See McIntyre, 1988:98–9.)

In some countries, a teacher is allocated a number of trainees and is given some time off teaching duties to supervise them. In Sri Lanka, as we have noted, such personnel are called *Field supervisors*. In some Francophone countries (e.g. Senegal), a similar function for the training of in-service teachers is carried out at district level by *Conseillers pedagogiques*, and at school level by *Animateurs pedagogiques*.

The most usual problem about using practising teachers in this way, as noted by Furlong and others (1988) with reference to the UK system, is that they are usually untrained in supervision and *formally* unqualified to do the job. They thus often feel insecure in performing supervisory functions, and may also lack status in this respect in the eyes of their colleagues. They do, however, have the advantage of closeness to the classroom situation. The lack of regular classroom experience is probably one of the most serious weaknesses in the credibility and effectiveness of many supervisors.

Whether or not such procedures are attractive or feasible in any given situation, there is sufficient evidence that, until now, it has very often been the case that the trainee's school experience and college training experience have not, in fact, been mutually supportive and complementary. By whatever means, measures have to be taken to ensure that both training agencies (the school and the college) are pulling in the same direction. The most obvious solutions are: (a) the establishment of adequate liaison machinery, and (b) the training and possibly even the formal qualification of teacher supervisors.

Progression in practical experience

In Chapter 6 (section 6.3) it was suggested that professional learning should be organised on a progressive cline from 'minimum risk/cost' to 'maximum risk/cost'. Obviously, the same principle should apply to practical experience. It is normal therefore to start practical experience with a period of observation, which gradually decreases as professional action is increased.

Observation does not simply mean watching classes. The trainee should have a practical experience 'folio' in which she responds to a number of tasks relating to various important aspects of school life. Included in this would be descriptions of the administrative structure of the school, disciplinary regulations and procedures, the layout of the school, the layout of a typical classroom (perhaps with photographs), the 'shadowing' of a particular student throughout a lesson or a day, and so on. In serial school experience this information can be timed to fit in with relevant inputs on school administration, learner psychology, or whatever.

Even when professional action is at a maximum it should never be equal to a full timetable. The trainee should always be allowed extra time for preparation, consultation and the performance of reflective tasks of various kinds, such as folio work, lesson evaluation, keeping a professional diary, and so on.

PERSONAL REVIEW

Do either (a) or (b).

a)   Imagine that you have a group of trainees who are going to be spending a day (or half day) observing language teaching classes. Devise an observation task sheet that will help them to structure their observation. (You will have to decide whether the trainees are pre-service or in-service as this may affect the nature of the tasks you will set.)

b)   Imagine that you have a group of trainees who are attending *either* a one-year post-graduate training course *or* the first year of a four-year B.Ed. course. They have serial school experience for one day per week in the first term, making ten days in all. Design a school experience folio or task sheet detailing the tasks you would expect them to perform during this part of their course.

Summary

Clinical supervision is a term which is sometimes used to mean a training mode and sometimes to mean a particular approach to that training mode. Here, I have suggested that the term clinical supervision is best kept for a training mode which involves a formative face-to-face interaction between a supervisor and a trainee or a teacher with reference to classroom teaching. Within that mode, the supervisor may wish to be, and may be expected to be, 'prescriptive', i.e. giving the trainee a clear indication of what the supervisor thinks she has done right or wrong. However, I have argued here that a more collaborative approach ought to be a goal of clinical supervision both for affective and for longer-term professional developmental reasons. Within the area of practical experience, I have suggested that the gradualistic, incremental approach to professional experiential learning presented in the last chapter should be implemented here also. This might involve a variety of different ways of organising practical experience (e.g. in terms of placement, one might have serial / block / internship), and also a variety of activities, of which professional action would be the most important, but not the only one. If schools are being used for the practical experience, then careful attention must also be given to liaison between the training institution and the schools.

PERSONAL REVIEW

Look again at the transcript at the end of the 'Personal review' on page 84 (initial presentation of a structure). How would you plan a clinical supervision session in relation to this extract?

In particular:

1. What further information would you want from the teacher?

2. What can you deduce from the evidence in the transcript about what the teacher's 'espoused theory' might be? Assuming that your deductions are correct, can you see any conflicts between her 'espoused theory' and her 'theory in use'? (For discussion of these terms, see page 119.)

3. What areas of the extract would you choose to discuss?

4. How would you handle the discussion?

5. What would you hope the outcome of the discussion to be?

6. Write a 'script' for the first five minutes of the supervisory dialogue imagining what you would say and how the teacher might respond. Compare your script with the scripts of other colleagues, if possible. You might find it interesting to act out some of the dialogues as a basis for discussion.

---

8   Assessment in teacher education

8.1   Overview

In this chapter some basic considerations in assessment for teacher education are briefly presented. Three main areas will be looked at: assignments, examinations and professional action. Far from being merely a 'necessary evil', assessment can play a positive role in a teacher education course, for example, by integrating various areas of the course, and by developing the trainees' powers of analysis and reflection.

8.2   Rationale for assessment

Assessment is obviously an important part of any course since it in fact determines what the students must do in order to gain the qualifications. Therefore, the *rationale* for the assessment scheme must be carefully thought through to make sure that assessment is actually helping the underlying aims and objectives of the course as a whole, and is not being used simply as a matter of tradition or routine. The following principles are suggested for consideration, as being principles which might well have a relevance to most courses:

1. *The assessment should be appropriately diagnostic and formative,* providing feedback to staff and trainees alike on the extent to which learning objectives are being realised, and on the existence of learning difficulties and the need for help and improvement.

2. The assessment should be *summative*: it should constitute a valid and reliable measure of academic and professional achievement.

3. The assessment should, at least, in part, act as an *integrating* device, serving to strengthen the overall coherence of the course by defining tasks which require the trainees to establish connections between components of the course. If there is a module of discourse analysis, for example, and also one on the teaching of reading, the two modules might be linked by asking trainees to do a project involving making a linguistic analysis of a text which is subsequently to be part of a reading comprehension lesson. Assessment which asks trainees to make connections across components will usually be in a

form which permits time for reflection, and also consultation where this is appropriate (i.e. it is unlikely to take the form of an unseen question in an examination).

4. In order to allow the trainees to show a range of expertise, and as a reflection of the varied demands of the course, forms of assessment should also be *varied*, and progressively more demanding as the course proceeds.

5. The *load* of assessment should be sufficient to yield adequate information (both to trainees and their tutors) on the trainees' progress, but not so heavy that they are denied sufficient time for reading and reflection.

6. The *distribution* of assessment should be such that the trainees are not under excessive pressure at certain points of the course and insufficiently stretched at others.

Not all of these principles may be relevant in every situation. For example, the third (the idea of using assessment as an integrating device) may not be desirable or feasible in a given situation.

8.3 Assignments

Just as there are different modes of teaching and learning, so it is probably appropriate that a variety of modes of assessment should be utilised, especially in a long course, so that the different aptitudes and abilities of trainees can be demonstrated. There will also be a relationship between different aims and different forms of feedback. Clearly, if one aim is to ensure that the trainees have memorised certain facts, and another that they can 'think on their feet' then these aims will probably require distinct and separate assessment.

Among the variety of types of assignments that are generally used are the following:

1. **Exercise**   An individual task carried out by the trainee drawing on content, studies and techniques that she has been introduced to.

2. **Presentation**   An individual task in which the trainee reads up material in a given area, and speaks about the topic before her group.

3. **Essay**   A piece of written work which shows that the trainee has done certain reading in a particular area, and is capable of a certain degree of analysis and judgement in that area.

4. **Review**   An individual task in which the trainee surveys and evaluates material available for teaching or learning a certain topic.

5. **Contract**   An independent piece of work, offering a very wide degree of choice, the format and content of which is negotiated between the tutor and each individual trainee.

6. **Project**   An independent piece of work, more sustained than an individual exercise, and demanding more in the way of autonomous study on the part of the trainee.

7. **Guided reading assignment** (GRA)   A type of assignment in which the trainee has to answer questions related to the reading which has been assigned. The questions may be simple comprehension questions; they may ask the trainee to relate the article to her own experience; they may ask the trainee to contrast the conclusions of this article with one previously read, and so on. This can be a cumulative form of assessment by which the trainee is introduced over time to certain key texts in various areas relevant to the subject being studied.

8. **Workbook**   A structured series of tasks carried out by the trainee, drawing on content, studies and techniques that she has been introduced to.

9. **Folio**   A logbook-type compilation of ongoing work, tasks and observations, usually done in the context of professional action, and including supervised and unsupervised items.

10. **Dissertation**   Extended treatment on a topic, showing some degree of scholarship.

PERSONAL REVIEW

Consider the range of assignments listed above. In the courses that you are familiar with, which of them are:

a)   commonly used
b)   occasionally used
c)   seldom or never used?

Are there any forms of assignments that you have found useful which have not been listed? What are they?

In connection with assignments, a point which has to be carefully considered is how far assignments like these should count towards the final qualification; in other words, the issue of how far *continuous assessment* should be used. Many people have felt that sole reliance on performance in an examination can lead to unreliable and invalid assessment. The reasons advanced for this view include the somewhat haphazard nature of 'good' or 'bad' examination papers, the narrow range of skills exhibited in examinations (especially traditional ones), unfairness to trainees who have different learning styles, the encouragement of steady application, and so on.

On the other hand, examinations can also be seen as being less prone to cheating, and as giving more responsibility to the trainee for organising her own learning. (For a discussion of these issues, see Beard and Hartley, 1984: Part Five.)

The answer once more will no doubt lie in carefully matching the aims and objectives of the course not only with the *form* of assessment used but also with the *weighting* given to the different forms of assessment. This has to be a matter for the professional judgement of individual tutors or the relevant course team.

8.4 Examinations

Examinations should be given in order to achieve certain objectives, and not as a matter of tradition or routine. In other words, one should be clear why certain aspects of performance are being tested by one kind of test and others by another. Among the abilities which examinations generally test are the trainees' ability to:

- understand, remember and discuss certain key information, concepts and skills which ought to be internalised as part of the trainees' experience of the course;
- deploy their knowledge and skills under reasonable pressure of time;
- argue and discuss concisely and persuasively within certain reasonable constraints of time and circumstance.

Examinations may be mounted in a variety of ways. In teacher education courses which are attempting to develop trainees' powers of observation and reflection, it is often a good idea to use video or audio based materials. For example, trainees can be asked to view or listen to part of a lesson and to make comments on certain aspects of the lesson. Other possibilities are seen or unseen questions, open-book approaches, and prepared tasks. These may be used according to whether one is expecting the trainees to demonstrate powers of recall of certain key information or the ability to think some problem through and answer it under controlled conditions. Individual oral examinations are time-consuming, but allow the opportunity to test areas of strength and weakness in an interactive way.

PERSONAL REVIEW

In your view, how much of the overall assessment should be dealt with by examinations in:

a) pre-service qualifications?
b) in-service qualifications?

What do you think of the use of seen questions and 'open-book' approaches in examinations? How far do you think audio-taped or video-taped lessons should be used for examining methodology? What sort of form would the resulting examination tasks take?

8.5   Professional action

Professional action is that part of practical experience in which the trainees have to demonstrate their capabilities as classroom practitioners (that is, in addition to other such necessary capabilities as analytical observation, selective data collection, etc.). This mostly concentrates on classroom performance, but also includes their ability to participate positively in the process of clinical supervision, and therefore includes their powers of self-evaluation. It is important to note that professional action assessment is formative as well as summative. Observation schedules should be devised not only to give a reliable and valid assessment of the trainee's performance, but also to act as a diagnostic instrument to improve that performance. Since it is difficult to be both a collaborative supervisor and an assessor, these functions should ideally be carried out by different people. If both functions have to be done by the same person, it should at least be clear to the trainee in which capacity (formative or summative) the supervisor is operating. In many professional action supervision programmes, there is a sequence of meetings, the earliest ones being formative and generally supportive, and the later ones summative. It is important for the trainee to know which sessions are to be summative. It is also useful to have some degree of flexibility; for example, the trainee may be assessed on the two best performances out of three, or whatever. Reliability is an acute problem in the summative assessment of professional action. At the barest minimum, trainees should be assessed on at least two occasions at different levels, and ideally by different assessors.

In some situations, it is normal for assessors of professional action to drop in on trainees unannounced and to assess them on 'how they really teach'. One can appreciate the thinking behind this: the prepared lesson may not, after all, be typical of the trainee's normal performance. However, this technique does seem to run counter to the usual conventions of examinations (if one assumes that the assessment of professional action is a kind of examination). Usually in examinations, candidates are given full details of the examination beforehand. Further, it must be recognised that a trainee is not in the position of a normal member of school staff: she might have been given a totally unsuitable class, or been inadequately briefed on the class, or asked to take a class with almost no warning. Assessment without due notification would, in these circumstances, seem to be a rather unfair way of proceeding.

PERSONAL REVIEW

Many tutors have to combine the role of adviser and assessor. Below is a list of qualities. Which do you think are appropriate to: (a) the tutor as adviser; (b) the tutor as assessor; (c) both roles; (d) neither role?

Qualities: patient, critical, fair, friendly, shrewd, conscientious, consistent, helpful, supportive, dispassionate/uninvolved, knowledgeable, courteous, collaborative, strict, prescriptive, taciturn, vigilant, honest, reserved, rigorous.

How would you reconcile the dual role of adviser and assessor?

8.6 Grading systems

Grading systems are very often decided by institutional regulations. Most institutions have a preferred form of grading which has to be applied across a range of courses. However, sometimes the course design team will have some freedom in deciding what form of grading they should apply, and this can be very problematic.

The first decision is whether one wishes to end up with a range of grades or whether one is satisfied with simply 'pass' or 'fail'. In some in-service courses, for example, one would be quite happy simply to be able to attest that the course participants have completed the course satisfactorily. In that case, a 'pass' or 'fail' or even perhaps simply a 'DP' (duly performed) will be sufficient. In other cases, a scale may be required, which may be a letter scale (A, B, C, D, E, etc.) or a numerical scale. Whichever of these is chosen, a decision will have to be made about how the pass grade or each grade of the scale, if it is a scale, is to be achieved. There are basically two approaches to this: by norm-referencing and by criterion-referencing.

Norm-referencing

The first way of doing this is by way of using as one's standard some kind of *norm*, i.e. an expectation derived from a typical range of performance. One kind of norm-referencing, for example, would be to decide that a certain percentage of candidates will pass the course each time, or that a certain percentage will be passed at each level. This would not usually be formally expressed as a specific percentage but may rather be in the form of an expectation (i.e. what one would normally expect). Thus, in a classified Honours degree the usual expectation is that a first class Honours pass will be exceptional, and that perhaps the majority of the passes will be in the second class Honours range, with a few third class Honours and perhaps an exceptional fail. This may be linked to some idea of an absolute standard of excellence being carried on from year to year. In other words, the assessment is based on the judgement of the internal and external examiners measured against some concept of absolute quality.

Norm-referenced tests ultimately derive from a statistical concept whereby the total number of candidates is assumed to fall into some kind of 'normal distribution', in which there will be a few very able people, a few very weak people, and the majority scattered at various points in the middle.

Criterion-referencing

A totally different approach is one which relates the pass or fail of a candidate to some explicitly stated *criteria*. The idea here is that the measurement of pass or fail is not done against some internalised judgement on the part of highly skilled examiners, but by some observable and measurable criteria which can be demonstrated in the candidates' performance. Tests like this are usually called *criterion-referenced* tests.

An example that is commonly used of a criterion-referenced test is a driving test. It is not sufficient that the would-be driver can do most things well (e.g. turning corners or parking), but has one thing that he or she cannot do (e.g. reversing). In order to pass the driving test the candidate must fulfil *all* the criteria specified by the test.

If we turn to teacher education, it is not impossible to devise criteria that we would expect of a good teacher. It is obvious, for example, that all teachers, and particularly language teachers, ought to be able to project their voices so that they can be heard in all parts of the class. We could therefore make this a necessary criterion for professional action (i.e. the trainee's performance while on teaching practice). Another criterion for a language teacher might be the ability to organise the class quickly and efficiently into groups for group work. We might also expect any language teacher to demonstrate the ability to design and use appropriate visual aids. There are many other examples of observable behaviour that we might expect a competent teacher to demonstrate successfully.

It must also be said, however, that establishing criteria in professional education is not such an easy matter as establishing criteria for skills such as driving a car or performing some mechanical operation. The criteria that have been specified above might be criticised because they include such words as 'quickly', 'efficiently', 'appropriate', which might allow different interpretations by different observers. Against this it might be argued that to limit assessment to what can be specified very clearly and unequivocally in behavioural terms is often to trivialise the procedure. We have frequently noted what a complex process teaching is, and it may well be the case that certain important aspects of professional action are not easily susceptible to specification by behaviouristic criteria.

A further complication is that very often courses require information not only on whether or not a candidate is capable of performing a certain skill, but also how *well* the skill is performed. Degrees of excellence are much more difficult to establish in a criterion-referenced way.

Nevertheless, the very effort to establish criteria may have the beneficial result of making the 'rules of the game' much more explicit both to those using the assessment instruments and to those whose performance is judged by such instruments. Thus, even if they are not fully satisfactory as criteria, tighter specifications of the salient aspects of the grading process may be very beneficial for everyone concerned, tutors and trainees alike. This is particularly the case if we wish to encourage reflection on performance, and also on the grading process itself.

PERSONAL REVIEW

Write down *ten* criteria for professional action that you would expect a competent teacher to be able to achieve. Try to make the criteria as 'observable' and 'objective' as possible. If you can, compare your criteria with those designed by other colleagues, and discuss the problems you encountered in trying to make the criteria observable and objective.

8.7   Assessment of professional action

It has been noted previously that professional action has a dual function: one important function being *formative*, i.e. for the purpose of training, and the other *evaluative*, i.e. for the purpose of assessment. Ideally the form of assessment used should help both. For most courses some form of observation schedule is used in order to standardise the assessment among various tutors, and also to give the candidate an idea of what is expected of her in her professional action assessment. There is a rich variety of such types of observation schedule available in language teaching. For a very stimulating and interesting range of methods of professional action by observation instruments, see the Royal Society of Arts / UCLES language teacher training syllabuses. These syllabuses are issued annually and include samples of the observation schedules used in the various programmes (addresses on page 135). It is a very useful exercise to look at these different schedules, to relate them to the programmes they are used for, and to think of possible applications of some of the techniques in one's own situation.

8.8   Assessment schedule

One of the most frequent complaints among trainees is the bunching of assignments at particular times. Sometimes this is unavoidable, but on some occasions it arises simply through lack of liaison among the contributing tutors. If possible, it is very useful for trainees to be given an assessment schedule which gives an indication of when major assignments are due. Alternatively, trainees can be given some kind of pro-forma on which to keep their own calendar of assignments so that they can pace their workload. Another frequent complaint is that certain books, articles, etc. are in heavy demand just before assignments are due. An inexpensive solution to this is to have a 'short-loan' system for such books and articles.

Summary

Assessment should not be a matter of tradition or routine only. Thought has to be given as to what the rationale of the assessment programme is, and, in particular, how far it matches the aims and objectives of the course. It is likely that a range of assessment techniques will be more appropriate than one or two techniques, and they should be appropriate to the kind of learning objectives they are intended to achieve. The assessment of professional action is particularly difficult to achieve so that it is valid and reliable. Although it is expensive in time, multiple assessment is probably necessary for fairness. Trainees should be given advance warning of assessments. Well-designed assessment schedules help to achieve both validity and reliability. Thought has to be given to management aspects of assessment, particularly in terms of timing and availability of resources.

PERSONAL REVIEW

On the following pages you will find copies of assessment schedules devised for two awards of the Royal Society of Arts Examination Board (RSA, Westwood Way, Coventry CV4 8HS; the first of these is now run in collaboration with the University of Cambridge Local Examinations Syndicate (UCLES, 1 Hills Road, Cambridge CB1 2EU). It should be noted that all the RSA and RSA/UCLES examinations are subject to constant evaluation, and the forms used here are not necessarily those currently in use. The forms are, of course, the copyright of the RSA and UCLES.

The first assessment schedule relates to the RSA/UCLES Diploma for Overseas Teachers of English; the second one relates to the RSA Diploma in the Teaching of English across the Curriculum in Multilingual Schools, i.e. UK schools which include children coming from different language backgrounds.

Bearing in mind their different objectives, compare the format of the two schedules. What points of similarity and difference do you see? What features seem to you to be noteworthy? How do these schedules compare with the assessment schedules you use in your own situation?

135

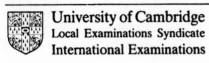 **University of Cambridge**
Local Examinations Syndicate
International Examinations

EXAMINATIONS BOARD

1 Hills Road   Cambridge   CB1 2EU   U.K.

Telephone: (U.K. Cambridge (0223) 61111   *Telegrams:* PROFICIENT Cambridge   *Telex:* 9401 2736=SYND G   *Facsimile:* 0223 460278
(International) + 44 223 61111

DIPLOMA FOR OVERSEAS TEACHERS OF ENGLISH   DOTE/4

Check List and Report on Practical Test

Candidate No.	Centre No.

Candidate's Name	
Place of Examination	Primary / Secondary / Further

Level of Class	Elementary		Intermediate		Advanced	
Average Age		Number of years of study of English				
Number in Class	Date				Time	

Any further relevant information about type, size, etc., of class and local conditions, e.g., aids and materials available.	
Aim of Lesson	

Personal Qualities	*Grade	Comments
Personality — 'Presence' general style		
Ability to establish rapport		
Voice-Audibility, ability to project		

Command of Language	*Grade	Comments
Correctness of Structure		
Vocabulary		
Register		
General Intelligibility including adequacy of pronunciation		
Fluency		
Sensitivity to pupils' level of language		

Preparation	*Grade	Comments
Lesson plan, balance and variety of activities, Timing		
Clarity, limitation and specification of aim		
Suitability of materials and methods for level and type of class		

Execution	*Grade	Comments
Techniques of class management		
Progress through the lesson, changes in activity, pace, etc		
Presentation of materials; Meaningful, motivated, contextualised, appropriately staged		
Questioning: graded, directed appropriate		
Controlled practice: choral-individual		
Ability to foster genuine language use		
Awareness and correction of errors		
Use of blackboard or equivalent		
Use of other aids		
Maintenance of interest		
Involvement and encouragement of learners		
Checking of learning		
Achievement of aims		
Ability to adapt and extemporize (if necessary)		
Understanding and handling of — Structure		
Understanding and handling of — Lexis		
Understanding and handling of — Phonology		
Handling of text, dialogue, etc., if presented		

Summarising Comments

Overall Assessment (Write A, B, C or D)*	Examiner's signature and name
	Name:
	Signed: Date:

EXAMINATIONS BOARD

DIPLOMA IN THE TEACHING OF ENGLISH ACROSS THE CURRICULUM IN MULTILINGUAL SCHOOLS

Westwood Way Coventry cv₄ ₈Hs Facsimile 0203 468080 Telephone 0203 470033

FINAL EXAMINATION: REPORT ON PRACTICAL TEST

Candidate's Name _____ Centre: _____

Place of examination – School: _____

Address: _____

Date: _____ Time: _____

SECTION 1   Preparation of the lesson

Using the notes provided by the candidate comment below on his/her preparation with reference to:

	S*	Comments
a) the relevance to the school curriculum and to the social/ cultural needs of the learners	☐	
b) the degree of integration with ongoing work	☐	
c) the analysis of the learning demands of the lesson	☐	
d) the learning objectives for this lesson	☐	
e) the analysis of the English language demands of the lesson	☐	
f) the linguistic objectives for this lesson and their relevance to the linguistic level of English language competence and needs of individual learners/ groups of learners	☐	
g) the appropriateness of the selection of materials	☐	
h) the appropriateness of planning of activities	☐	
i) the appropriateness of the organisation of the class	☐	
j) an overall anti-racist perspective	☐	

* Satisfactory   Tick if appropriate and comment.

138

SECTION 2   Execution and management of the lesson

Comment on the candidate's ability to support the English language
development of bilingual learners by providing:

	S*	Comments

a) clear instructions and models
   of English language usage

b) effective teacher/pupil interaction

c) effective organisation and
   management of the whole class

d) a variety of activities

e) effective materials

f) support for understanding

g) opportunities for learners to
   apply their existing skills
   and knowledge

h) opportunities for developing
   English language use

i) opportunities for peer group
   interaction

j) effective monitoring of learning

k) a sensitive environment for
   individual learners and their
   communicative needs

SECTION 3   Candidate's evaluation of the lesson

Comment on how the candidate evaluated her/his own lesson after the
assessment in terms of the objectives set out in the notes.   (N.B.
The candidate is not expected to write, nor to submit later, an
evaluation of the lesson)

SECTION 4 Overall comments with reference to the following criteria for the assessment of practical teaching

---

At pass level candidates must:

(i)   in their notes
(a) show an understanding of the language and learning demands of the lesson and relate these to the ages, stages of development and the language and learning needs of the bilingual pupils in the class.

(b) present a lesson, fitting into a scheme of work within the framework of the mainstream curriculum, which will support the English language development of the bilingual children

(ii)   in the execution of the lesson shwo their ability to organise, monitor and genuinely support language and learning over a range of activities which allow the bilingual pupils to exploit their existing skills and knowledge.

In addition at a distinction level candidates must:

(i)   in their notes

(a) show a clear analysis of the language and learning demands of the lesson and show how these relate to the stated language and learning needs of the children.

(b) show a clear understanding of the processes of language acquisition in terms of the development of the lesson and the imaginative use of the activities and materials employed.

(ii)   show an outstanding ability to execute the lesson in terms of (a) organisation, (b) activities, (c) the exploitation of the bilingual pupils' learning and language potential and (d) sensitivity to the needs of individual pupils in the class.

SECTION 5 Final assessment

FINAL ASSESSMENT(Write PASS/FAIL*/DISTINCTION*) _____

* Reasons for award of a FAIL or DISTINCTION assessment:

Assessors are reminded that they must return this form, ET22(M) and the accompanying teaching notes within one week of the practical test.

Name of Assessor: _____

Signature: _____ Date: _____

---

9 Course design and assessment: Checklist and case study

9.1 Overview

The intention of this chapter is to provide you with a checklist of issues which it might be worthwhile taking into consideration when designing foreign language teacher education courses. To illustrate the points at issue, I will use a case study approach. The case study will be frequently referred to and parts of it will be reproduced throughout the chapter as in 'Case study figure 1' etc. The case study is a four-year pre-service Honours Bachelor of Education Degree in Teaching English to Speakers of Other Languages (B.Ed.(Hons) TESOL). The trainees would come in at about eighteen years old, having done a two-year pre-university course in the UK. They are non-native speakers of English but studying in the UK. It should be clear, hopefully, that the case study is presented simply as stimulus for reflection and discussion, and not as a blueprint or model.

There are various ways in which course-planning can be organised. In references to the case study it will be assumed that the planning is being done by a group of people called 'the course team'.

9.2 Rationale

Need for a rationale

Every course should have a *rationale*, that is to say a reasoned explanation of what kind of course it is, and why it has been designed in the way it has. It is also important to specify the training and educational philosophy underpinning the course, whether it be reflective practice or whatever. The rationale may include elements similar to those listed below.

Type of course

What is the basic type of the course? Is it pre-service or in-service? Is it a four-year B.Ed. degree, a one-year Postgraduate Certificate, or an RSA

Diploma course? Is it a short intensive course or a full-time course, to be studied straight through? Is it a credit accumulation course which may be picked up for a while and then left for a while and then picked up again? Is it a sandwich course which can be interrupted by full-time service and then taken up again? The answers to these questions will relate to other factors listed below, such as the resources, target population, and so on.

Resources

The course type may relate to some extent to the resources required. How is the resource entitlement of a course decided? Is it a ratio of so many trainees to each tutor? For example, the recruitment of 150 trainees, at a staff–trainee ratio of 1:10, will provide an 'entitlement' of fifteen tutors. The course planner has to know how many sessions a tutor normally teaches and try to relate the course demands to the number of hours available.

Target population

What kind of trainee is the course designed for? Is it intended to capture pre-service trainees in the form of school leavers? Is it intended perhaps to attract in-service teachers who want to improve their qualifications? Or is it simply for teachers who need a refresher course to get new ideas? Is it perhaps designed for a group of trainees who have very different backgrounds and needs? What form of marketing is necessary to attract trainees? Will there be an open day, for example, when would-be trainees can find out about the institution and talk to members of staff?

Admission requirements

What are the minimum or normal academic professional qualifications expected of those being enrolled on the course? Is there going to be some form of admissions procedure, for example, by competitive examination, by interview, by reference from the school or employee, or by some recruitment procedures specific to the profession involving, perhaps, the demonstration of teaching aptitude, the ability to work with others in groups, etc.?

Need for the course

What evidence is there concerning the need for the course? Are there public policy statements, for example? Is the course perhaps related to some major programme of innovation or reform? If so, how is the course intended to fit into such a programme?

9.3 Aims and objectives

Aims

In broad terms, what is the course intended to achieve? For an example of the course aims in the case study, see Case study figure 1.

PERSONAL REVIEW

Look at the course aims in Case study figure 1. How many of the aims would relate to trainees on a pre-service course in your context? Are there any aims missing which you would insist on for trainees in your context? Are there any aims which would not seem to you to be necessary?

Case study figure 1

Aims

1. To develop in the trainees an understanding of the principles of language teaching based on current theories concerning language acquisition, linguistics (with special reference to English), pedagogics, and the sociology and psychology of learning;

2. To show the trainees how to apply these principles to their future professional role and, in particular, to the Teaching of English to Speakers of Other Languages (TESOL);

3. To afford the trainees the opportunity to practise the teaching of English in a controlled way so that they will emerge as confident and competent classroom teachers;

4. To develop further the trainees' competence and fluency in English so that they can communicate effectively as teachers, and also themselves become good models of communication in the target language;

5. To sensitise the trainees to the use of English for literary purposes by the study of appropriate texts;

(continued)

6. To expand the trainees' range of academic experience and professional expertise by training them in a subsidiary subject area, and to demonstrate the links between the subsidiary subject and the study of language across the curriculum;

7. To foster in the trainees the general intellectual capacities commensurate with the developing professional role of the teacher under the changing circumstances of their future careers, and in particular the capacity to reflect in a structured way on their classroom practice;

8. To develop in the trainees the kind of professional perspective which enables them to locate their teaching in the wider context of the school and the community;

9. To develop in the trainees powers of self-evaluation linked with an orientation towards autonomous learning which will enable them to improve their abilities as teachers once their initial training is over.

Case study figure 1 (contd.)

Objectives

Objectives should normally be related to aims, but should be more specific and ideally measurable in some way. Successful trainees should be able to demonstrate that they have achieved the objectives, and indeed should be required to do so through the assessment procedures. For an example of the course objectives from the case study, see Case study figure 2.

PERSONAL REVIEW

How do the case study objectives relate to the aims stated in Case study figure 1? Are all the objectives 'measurable'? Are they all worthwhile, or are some of them trivial? Are there objectives that are not mentioned here which would be important to pre-service trainees in your situation?

Objectives

Trainees will be expected to demonstrate:

1. The ability to plan, implement and evaluate appropriate learning experiences for their students;

2. A sound grasp of the theory of language teaching methodology so that they will not only understand what methods are appropriate in a given situation but also why they are appropriate;

3. A sufficient understanding of the system of the English language to prepare language teaching materials on a sound basis;

4. The ability to use and, where necessary, adapt language texts commonly in use in [target country];

5. The ability to modify their teaching strategies in the light of self-evaluation;

6. A good model of English in all the necessary communicative situations involved in language teaching;

7. The ability to appreciate a literary text of an appropriate level and subject matter and to explain the basis of their appreciation;

8. The ability to analyse the social, psychological and educational contexts in which teaching and learning take place;

9. The ability to undertake sustained independent academic work.

Case study figure 2

9.4 Principles relating to the overall design of the course

It is important that the course team (i.e. those responsible for planning the course) should consider what guiding principles it intends to espouse in designing the course. Of their nature, these principles will be rather broad in scope and will relate to the general nature of the qualities that the course should possess. The principles decided upon will obviously have to be complementary to the course aims and objectives.

PERSONAL REVIEW

Look at the design principles from the case study in Case study figure 3. How important, acceptable and relevant would these seem in your own situation?

Basic principles relating to the overall design of the course

The qualities that the course planning team feels are necessary in a course of this kind are as follows:

1. The course should be **relevant** to the educational and professional needs of the target population, and to the needs of the community which they will serve as professional educators;

2. As a pre-service qualification of Honours standard and as the culmination of the trainees' educational experience before taking up their professional careers, the course should be **broadly educative** to a high level, in terms of the trainees' personal and intellectual development;

3. At the same time, the course should be **fully professional,** in that it prepares the trainees for a particular profession: it must therefore ensure that its graduates are fully competent to assume their responsibilities in the career of their choice, and, further, it must look beyond its own timespan to the continuing development of its graduates as autonomous professionals and 'reflective practitioners';

4. As a corollary of 2 and 3 above, the course should lead trainees to greater **autonomy** by allowing them increasing independence of action as the course progresses;

5. The course should be **culturally broadening,** in that it should capitalise, as far as possible, on the trainees' presence in Britain to broaden their cultural horizons, while at the same time completely respecting the integrity of their own culture.

Case study figure 3

9.5 Structure of the course

Thought will obviously have to be given to the structure of the course. What are the major strands in the course? How are the units of instruction organised, for example, is the course organised in terms of units of so many hours each? What are the main subject areas going to be? How do they relate to one another? How is practical experience going to be organised: serially, by blocks of experience, internship, or by some combination of these? For outline information on the basic structure of the case study, see Case study figure 4.

PERSONAL REVIEW

Look at the information given in Case study figure 4 about the structure of the case study. Do you agree with the general way of organising the main elements of the course? Is there anything that strikes you as unusual about the choice of subjects to be taught or the way that they are grouped together? Are there any subjects not listed which you think ought to be featured? What do you think about the amount of time that is devoted to school experience? Bearing in mind the fact that the course is being taught in one country and relates to education in another, what do you think of the way in which the school experience has been organised?

Case study figure 4

Outline course structure

The course consists of four major strands: (1) the Curricular areas; (2) the Theory and practice of teaching and learning; (3) School experience, and (4) Academic counselling.

Curricular areas

The Curricular areas cover two main subjects: English studies and the subsidiary subject.

English studies comprises:
a) Units related to the study of language (including the system of English, discourse in English, varieties of English and the analysis of spoken and written English).
b) Units relating to the study of literature.

Theory and practice of teaching and learning (TPTL)

TPTL covers two main areas: *Learning and the learner* and *Methodology*.

1. *Learning and the learner* comprises the following units:
   The teacher in the educational system
   Psychology of learning
   Psychology of second language learning
   Language learning and society
   Social context of the classroom
   Analysis of classroom experience
   Open learning, individual learning and self-direction
   Computer studies:
      Computer awareness
      Computer assisted learning I
      Computer assisted learning II

2. *Methodology* comprises TESOL Methodology and teaching of the subsidiary subject. TESOL Methodology is the major subject in the degree.

(continued)

School experience (SE)

There will be 24 weeks of SE (with an extra two weeks' block SE for weak students), divided as follows:

Time	Length	Location
Yr 1 (September)	1 wk (Block)	Home country
(Through year)	3 wks (Serial)	UK
Yr 2 (Term 2)	5 wks (Block)	UK
Yr 3 (September)	2 wks (Block)*	UK *Remedial only
(Term 3)	12 wks (Block)	Home country
Yr 4 (Through year)	3 wks (Serial)	UK

Academic counselling

Academic counselling is composed of four 30-hour units (one unit for each year), provided on a one-hour-per-week basis. In addition, in the final year there are ten individual tutorials devoted to the professional project, most of which will be taken by the Professional Project Supervisor.

Case study figure 4 (contd.)

9.6 Progression

Is it envisaged that there will be some kind of progression in the course, so that the nature and quality of work being done at the end of the course pose greater academic and professional challenges from that being done at the beginning? It is very common, for example, for professional courses to have a graded, shallow-ended approach so that the trainee teacher can gradually be exposed to the more 'risky' or 'costly' experiential aspects of professional practice. (This issue was discussed in Chapter 6, in sections 6.2 and 6.3.) If this approach is part of the philosophy of the course then it might be expected that it will be reflected in the course design.

The model of progression for the case study is summarised in Case study figure 5. It will be seen that in the case study the course is organised in terms of a graded shallow-ended approach, and this is articulated in terms of a three-cycle progression. In length the three cycles are divided as follows:

Cycle 1 – Year 1
Cycle 2 – Year 2
            Terms 1 and 2 of Year 3
Cycle 3 – Term 3 of Year 3
            Year 4

In the first two cycles, the progression is expressed in different but complementary ways with respect to the curricular areas on the one hand and the theory and practice of teaching and learning with school experience on the other. In the third cycle all three strands are integrated. This is shown in Case study figure 5.

PERSONAL REVIEW

Look at the model of progression that is suggested in Case study figure 5. Does this seem to you a sensible way of organising progression in a four-year degree? Would you have wished to make some changes or perhaps have a totally different approach to progression? How does it compare with other modes of progression in teacher education courses that you are familiar with?

F

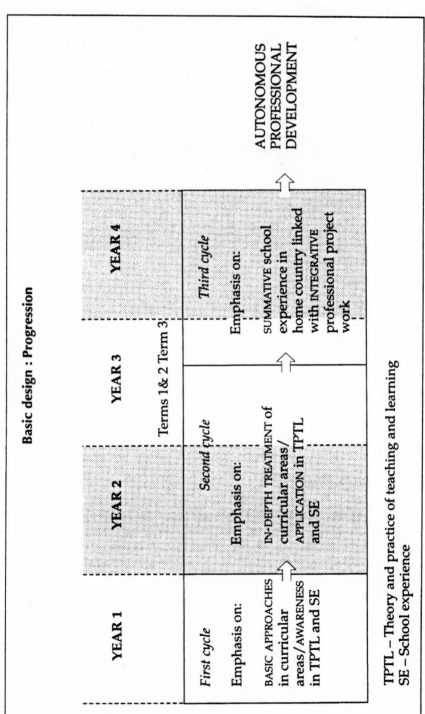

Basic design : Progression

	YEAR 1	YEAR 2	YEAR 3	YEAR 4
			Terms 1& 2 Term 3	

First cycle

Emphasis on:

BASIC APPROACHES in curricular areas / AWARENESS in TPTL and SE

Second cycle

Emphasis on:

IN-DEPTH TREATMENT of curricular areas / APPLICATION in TPTL and SE

Third cycle

Emphasis on:

SUMMATIVE school experience in home country linked with INTEGRATIVE professional project work

AUTONOMOUS
PROFESSIONAL
DEVELOPMENT

TPTL – Theory and practice of teaching and learning
SE – School experience

Case study figure 5

9.7 Coherence

One of the basic decisions that has to be made about any course of professional education is how far the different elements of the course are going to *cohere* with one another. In other words, how far are the course designers going to try and ensure that the different elements in the course will be seen as relevant to one another and forming a coherent training experience?

It is generally accepted that there are two kinds of coherence in a course, which we might call *synchronic coherence* and *sequential coherence.*

Synchronic coherence relates to the subjects as they are experienced by the trainee within each term or each year. In other words, what tends to happen in most courses is that the trainee experiences a number of inputs at roughly the same time. Thus, for example, she may attend a psychology lecture on Monday and go to a methodology lecture on the same day or perhaps the following day, and so on. Synchronic coherence asks the question: how far have these experiences been designed to dovetail and be complementary to one another as the course goes on?

Sequential coherence is concerned with how, for example, the teaching of a subject at the beginning of the course relates to the teaching of the same subject later in the course, and how the experience of the various subjects at the beginning relates to the experience of the various subjects later in terms of ongoing professional development.

There are various ways in which synchronic and sequential coherence can be achieved. One way is by breaking down the barriers between subjects. For example, the traditional 'professional subject' disciplines of psychology, sociology, etc. may be abolished and a new subject put in their place which cuts across them. Another very powerful method of achieving coherence is through assessment. If the various elements of a course have a common assessment then it will be necessary for those providing the input to collaborate at least to the extent of preparing a common examination paper perhaps, or common tasks and assignments.

Case study figure 6 shows how an attempt was made to achieve coherence in the case study through the elements of the basic design. You will see that there is intended to be a reciprocal relationship between school experience and the Theory and Practice of Teaching and Learning (TPTL). It is not intended that the trainees should merely apply what they have learned in TPTL to their school experience. It is also intended that the school experience should feed back into and inform the trainees' understanding of Learning and the Learner and Methodology. Again one of the possible kinds of machinery for achieving this is by means of appropriate forms of course work and assessment.

PERSONAL REVIEW

Look at the plan for coherence within the case study and think about the organisational and personal problems which are involved in such a design. How would one go about making these relationships 'real' and not just a theoretical ideal? Relating it to personal experience, consider whether such a pattern of coherence seems desirable in any context that you know about or whether some other more effective way of achieving the same aim in your own context might be achieved.

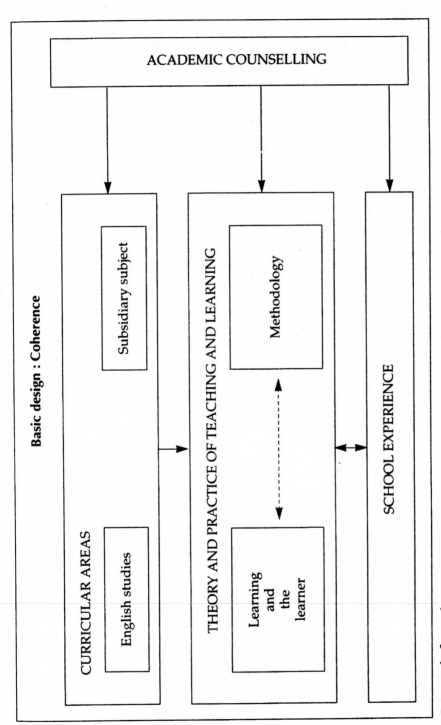

Basic design : Coherence

ACADEMIC COUNSELLING

CURRICULAR AREAS

English studies

Subsidiary subject

THEORY AND PRACTICE OF TEACHING AND LEARNING

Methodology

Learning
and
the
learner

SCHOOL EXPERIENCE

Case study figure 6

9.8 Methodology

The methodology of teacher education has a dual function: one function is of course to inform and teach the trainee both in terms of received knowledge and experiential knowledge. Another important function, however, is also to provide exemplification of good teaching practice. This might very well mean that a variety of teaching modes should be used, as suggested in Chapter 3. In the case study, the range of teaching methods included: lectures, tutorials, seminars, workshops, practical work, microteaching and field work.

9.9 Patterns of assessment

Trainees should be clear about what the pattern of assessment is. For example, they should know which elements are to be assessed by assignments and which by exam. If there are to be integrated assignments or exams (i.e. where more than one subject is to be assessed by the same assignment or exam) then this should be made clear. The pattern of assessment should also reveal whether the modes of assessment are properly varied and balanced.

The pattern of assessment will not, of course, tell the trainees all they need to know. They will also have to know the length of assignments, due dates, and so on, perhaps in the form of an assessment schedule at the beginning of each year (see section 8.8 in the previous chapter).

PERSONAL REVIEW

Look at the pattern of assessment displayed in Case study figure 7. What do you think of this pattern of assessment? Observe the number of integrated assignments: what is this intended to achieve? What practical problems do you foresee? Are there any potential practical benefits? Do they outweigh the disadvantages?

Pattern of assessment

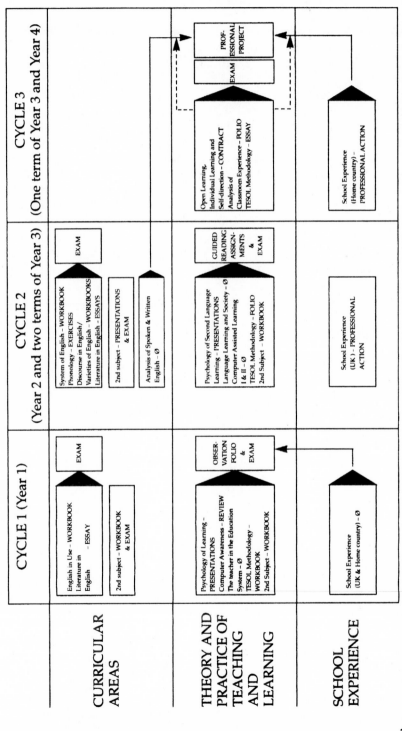

	CYCLE 1 (Year 1)	CYCLE 2 (Year 2 and two terms of Year 3)	CYCLE 3 (One term of Year 3 and Year 4)
CURRICULAR AREAS	English in Use – WORKBOOK Literature in English – ESSAY EXAM 2nd subject – WORKBOOK & EXAM	System of English – WORKBOOK Phonology – EXERCISES Discourse in English / Varieties of English – WORKBOOKS Literature in English – ESSAYS EXAM 2nd subject – PRESENTATIONS & EXAM Analysis of Spoken & Written English – Ø	
THEORY AND PRACTICE OF TEACHING AND LEARNING	Psychology of Learning – PRESENTATIONS Computer Awareness – REVIEW The teacher in the Education System – Ø TESOL Methodology – WORKBOOK 2nd Subject – WORKBOOK OBSER-VATION FOLIO & EXAM	Psychology of Second Language Learning – PRESENTATIONS Language Learning and Society – Ø Computer Assisted Learning I & II – Ø TESOL Methodology – FOLIO 2nd Subject – WORKBOOK GUIDED READING ASSIGN-MENTS & EXAM	Open Learning, Individual Learning and Self-direction – CONTRACT Analysis of Classroom Experience – FOLIO TESOL Methodology – ESSAY EXAM PROF-ESSIONAL PROJECT
SCHOOL EXPERIENCE	School Experience (UK & Home country) – Ø	School Experience (UK) – PROFESSIONAL ACTION	School Experience (Home country) – PROFESSIONAL ACTION

KEY: ▲ – INTEGRATED ASSESSMENT   Ø – NOT SEPARATELY ASSESSED   ---▶ ACADEMIC SUPPORT

Case study figure 7

157

9.10   Assignment: Grading by criteria

It was noted in the previous chapter that the use of criteria had become popular, partly as a means of making more explicit to the tutor and trainee alike what criteria are actually being invoked in a particular assessment.

In the case study, the course team were faced with the problem of working out a grading scheme for assessment which would work on a five-point scale A – E, where E was a fail. This scheme had to be able to work for the whole range of assignments and examinations, with the sole exception of professional action, which is discussed later in this chapter. The team decided to go for a 'profile' which would give a grade to the trainee in one or more of five criterion areas, *where these were relevant*. Thus, if the assignment did not call for 'primary data collection' (see Case study figure 8), this would not be marked. The grades would be added up and averaged by giving each grade a value (e.g. A = 5, B = 4, etc.). It would be possible to 'weight' certain criterion areas, for example, 'content, analysis and discussion' could be given a weighting of double value (i.e. × 2).

PERSONAL REVIEW

Look at the grading scheme in Case study figure 8, where the second criterion area has been described in full. How helpful or otherwise do you think such a scheme is to the trainee and/or the tutor? How valid are the 'criteria'? How would you set about writing criteria for grades A – E for the other criterion areas? Does this rather elaborate scheme achieve anything that could not be achieved with subjective grading and comments?

Assignment profile

Name _____

Date _____

Title of assignment _____

PROFILE

	CRITERION AREA	GRADE	COMMENTS
1.	LANGUAGE AND DISCOURSE ORGANISATION		
2.	CONTENT, ANALYSIS AND DISCUSSION		
3.	USE OF READING AND OTHER SOURCES		
4.	PRIMARY DATA COLLECTION		
5.	PRACTICAL AREAS AND APPLICATION		

OVERALL GRADE ☐

COMMENTS

Case study figure 8   *(continued)*

2. CONTENT, ANALYSIS AND DISCUSSION: Clarity, conviction, consistency, logicality, relevance

A	B	C	D	E
Content is relevant, with consistent indications of innovativeness/ originality.	Content is relevant, with occasional elements of innovativeness/ originality. Errors of fact are trivial.	Content is relevant and adequate to the purpose. Few errors of any significance.	Content is by and large relevant and sufficient for the purpose. Some significant factual errors, but not misleading overall.	Content is insufficient and/or irrelevant. Many errors of fact.
Errors of fact are few and trivial.	Good powers of analysis and discussion.	Can analyse material at more than a superficial level and discuss it clearly, sensibly and logically. Argument is coherent and consistent, and usually acceptable.	Can analyse material, albeit at a fairly superficial level and discuss it clearly and sensibly. Does not make obvious errors of logic.	Few or no powers of analysis.
Evidence of well-developed powers of analysis and discussion.	Arguments are logical, clear, consistent and usually convincing.	Overall effect is competent.	Argument is reasonably consistent.	Argument is inconsistent, illogical and unconvincing.
Arguments handled vigorously and in a logical, lucid and convincing way.	Overall effect is substantial and helpful to understanding of the topic.		Overall effect is of someone not completely in command of material, but the general effect is not trivial or misleading either.	It is often not clear what the point of the argument is.
Overall effect is substantial and even (at this level) insightful.				Overall effect is trivial, and/or misleading, and/or irrelevant.

Case study figure 8 (contd.)

9.11 Professional action observation schedule

We have already noted (section 8.5 above) that the assessment of professional action should usually have a formative as well as an evaluative function. It should therefore be informative to the trainee, and so it helps if the criteria for the judgement are reasonably explicit.

As we also noted in the previous chapter, the assessment generally should be based on some coherent rationale which is in accord with the aims and objectives of the course.

The format of the assessment should make it accessible both to the trainee and to the supervisor who has to use it. Let us now see how these considerations were tackled in the case study material.

The 'Professional action observation schedule' in Case study figure 9 is intended to be used by putting a tick in the appropriate column under *outstanding, competent, inadequate,* or *insufficient information*. There is also a 'summary grade' for each of the four main areas of *personal qualities, planning, implementation* and *evaluation*. These are graded on a three-point scale of D (Distinction), P (Pass) or F (Fail). The criteria for the grades are also provided; for example, the criteria for the first category (Presence/style) go as follows:

Outstanding: Commanding presence; individual and positive teaching style.
Competent: Good presence; no serious defects (e.g. over-mannered) in teaching style.
Inadequate: Personality has little or no impact; teaching style is irritating, boring, etc.

For the tenth category (Questioning techniques) the criteria are:

Outstanding: Questioning is highly relevant, varied and stimulating to the learners.
Competent: Questioning is appropriate, clear and keeps the lesson moving forward.
Inadequate: Questioning is random, irrelevant, unclear, monotonous.

PERSONAL REVIEW

How far do you agree with the areas for professional action that have been highlighted in the schedule Case study figure 9? What are the similarities or differences between this schedule and those which were documented at the end of Chapter 8? Pick two or three of the categories, and see how problematic or otherwise it is to write criteria for the three levels: *outstanding, competent* and *inadequate*.

Professional action observation schedule

Trainee's name _____   Class _____
Observer's name _____   School _____
                                       Date _____
                                       Time _____

	Summary grades	Outstanding	Competent	Inadequate	Insufficient information	Trainee's familiarity with class:
PERSONAL QUALITIES						**FURTHER COMMENT**
1. Presence/style						
2. Voice						
3. Rapport						
PLANNING						
4. Shape and balance of activities						
5. Aims and objectives: specification						
6. Aids/materials/methods: suitability						
7. Anticipation of difficulties						
IMPLEMENTATION						
8. General class management						
9. Introduction and presentation techniques						
10. Questioning techniques						
11. Language skills development						
12. Teaching aids						
13. Teaching materials						
14. Awareness/treatment of error						
15. Smoothness of flow						
16. Ability to adapt/extemporise						
17. T's language: model/level						
18. Achievement of aims/objectives						
EVALUATION						
19. Ability to evaluate own performance						
20. Ability to respond constructively to evaluation from others						
OVERALL GRADE (D/P/F)						

Case study figure 9

9.12 Appeals procedure

It will be necessary in many courses to establish an appeals procedure which will, on the one hand, be clearly just and equitable to any trainee who has a grievance, but on the other hand should not be too clumsy or time-consuming to put into operation.

9.13 Course evaluation

Thought will also have to be given as to how the course is to be evaluated. There will of course be several ways in which this could be done. One source of evaluation will obviously be the trainees themselves, and some procedure should be instituted whereby trainees are able to give clearly and, if necessary, anonymously their views on the course as it affects them. There may also be provision for direct representation on course committees so that the trainees can see that their complaints, if they have any, are being given due consideration. The tutors' comments will also be valuable, and some way will have to be established to consider these, perhaps by the establishment of a course committee consisting of the tutors on the course.

Another important aspect of evaluation might be the appointment of an external examiner, or more than one, who will have the power to make recommendations to the course committee and to the training institution. It might also be that the clients, in the form of members of the public or schools, or perhaps representatives of the Ministry of Education, should be represented on course committees to ensure a balance of views, and also to ensure that the course does not become too inward-looking and perhaps self-serving.

The course committee might be required to produce at regular intervals some kind of formal evaluation under certain prescribed categories, which would be considered by the training institution in its own review of the provision of its courses.

9.14 Other issues

Although this checklist has been a long one it has not, of course, covered all possible aspects of a teacher education course, especially a substantial one. There are many other issues, such as welfare activities, course induction procedures, and so on, which have not been covered here. It goes without saying that at a more specific level there would have to be a description of the individual course units which would probably include: the *length* of the unit; the *rationale* of the unit, justifying the unit's place in the curriculum and also discussing its relationship to other units; *objectives* of the unit; *methods of learning* (whether by lecture, tutorial, seminars, etc.); the *main topics* to be covered; a *bibliography*; and the *methods of assessment* for the unit.

Summary

This chapter has comprised a checklist of some factors that might well be taken into account in planning a teacher education course and in preparing the necessary documentation for such a course. Any teacher education course should be based on a clearly conceptualised and articulated rationale. The various aspects of the course should relate in some specified way to this rationale. The basic principles of the course design should be articulated and, in particular, attention should be paid to such issues as the structure of the course, the methodology of the course, course coherence, course progression, and assessment. Special attention should be paid to the role and organisation of practical experience. Lastly, thought should be given to management issues such as course evaluation, the appeals procedure, etc.

PERSONAL REVIEW

Take any aspect of the case study (Case study figures 1–9) and, for a course that you are familiar with, or a course that you are reviewing or would like to design, devise your own specifications (including documentation where appropriate) for the target course. You might find it useful to compare and contrast your specification with the specification given for the case study and discuss with colleagues any similarities and differences.

Concluding remarks

The basic assumption of this book is that it is helpful, and perhaps even necessary, to have some kind of rationale or set of organising principles for foreign language teacher education. Without such a rationale, foreign language teacher education programmes can become simply a grouping of inputs or activities adopted for a variety of reasons, implemented in a variety of ways, and therefore unlikely to form a coherent training experience. There is nothing necessarily constraining about such a rationale. If the organising principles are soundly based, then they should be robust enough to be adapted to a wide range of local contexts. Moreover, it could be argued that what is truly constraining is to be the prisoner of unexamined traditions of teacher education which may never have had any real professional validity, or which may have lost whatever validity they once had through the passage of time.

Clearly, therefore, many different rationales are possible. The one which has been presented here is that of 'reflective practice' or 'the teacher as reflective practitioner', which, for convenience, we have called 'the reflective approach'. There are several reasons for this approach being given serious consideration by those concerned with language teaching. One is that, while it is probably not yet the dominant philosophy of teacher education, it has already gained very wide acceptance in teacher education circles. Secondly, it derives from the study of how professionals *in general* learn their professions, and is therefore grounded on a broad base of professional knowledge and experience. Thirdly, it is consistent with, and complementary to, other developments currently taking place in language teaching classrooms, with their emphasis on the learner, and on learner training. (See, for example, *Learning to Learn English: A Course in Learner Training* by Ellis and Sinclair, 1989.) Techniques employed by these authors include: awareness activities, self-assessment, introspection, experimentation and reflection.

Not all professionals automatically continue to develop in the practice of their profession, nor do they all develop to the same high level of expertise. The inference from this might be that the process of reflection cannot be taken for granted, that one cannot assume that it will develop simply by doing the job. It follows that it would seem advisable for trainees' powers of reflection to be facilitated and developed through the training process. Various techniques have been proposed in this book for achieving this requirement, notably heuristic and experiential learning procedures, classroom observation, microteaching and collaborative clinical supervision.

An important aim of the reflective approach to teacher education is to empower teachers to manage their own professional development. Surely few things could be more conducive to raising the standards of teaching than a cadre of teachers who have the skills, ability and motivation to develop their practice. Realistically, it must be admitted that in many cases this will not happen. This could be for a variety of reasons: because of low morale, lack of inducement or reward, or simply because it does not square with the prevailing view of what is entailed by the job description of the classroom teacher.

A second aim of this approach is to enable teachers to be more effective partners in innovation. In many situations teachers themselves are not recognised as possible agents of change, even in a very limited way: innovation is always a top-down affair. Such innovation very often does not have its maximum impact because the teaching force is largely passive and reactive. To overcome this, two kinds of change are necessary. The first is in management style and procedures. The second is a change in the teachers' perception of their role. If foundations have been laid where, during their training period, at least some teachers have had an opportunity to be reflective and collaborative, then it might be possible for their professional expertise to be harnessed to implement innovation more effectively.

The role proposed here, of the language teacher as reflective practitioner, is a very demanding one. There are many understandable reasons why such a role might be avoided or declined. Nevertheless, it could be strongly argued that, if we as language teaching professionals do not rise to this challenge, the status of teaching as a *profession*, already under attack from many quarters, will be even more at risk.

Some suggestions for further reading

Key texts are Donald Schön's *The Reflective Practitioner: How Professionals Think in Action* (1983), and his more recent *Educating the Reflective Practitioner: Toward a New Design for Teaching and Learning in the Professions* (1987). Some very helpful articles will be found in D. Boud, R. Keogh and D. Walker (eds.) *Reflection – Turning Experience into Learning* (1985).

On teacher training for language teaching, there is an extremely useful survey article by Donard Britten called 'Teacher Training in ELT' (1985). A very good example of the practical application of heuristic and experiential learning techniques is Adrian Doff's *Teach English: A Training Course for Teachers* (1988).

On the topic of the teacher as researcher, two very useful guides to action research for the teacher are: David Hopkins' *A Teacher's Guide to Classroom Research* (1985) and Rob Walker's *Doing Research: A Handbook for Teachers* (1985). Both these books are reasonably 'user-friendly', but of the two, Hopkins' book is probably the simpler in its treatment of the topic and Walker's the more comprehensive.

The best book that I have read on microteaching written in the context of a developing country situation is unfortunately so far available only in French: A. Altet and J. D. Britten (1983) *Micro-enseignement et formation des enseignants* (Paris: Presses Universitaires de France). For an account of recent developments in microteaching, B. McGarvey and D. Swallow *Microteaching in Teacher Education and Training* (1986) is essential reading. E. Perrott's *Effective Teaching* (1982) is a good example of the microteaching approach in action.

For supervision, T. J. Sergiovanni and R. J. Starratt *Supervision: Human Perspectives* (3rd ed., 1983) is a basic text. It is very much rooted in the American tradition of supervision, naturally, and is therefore not always easy to relate to other situations, but it is authoritative and extremely informative. Good expositions of the collaborative and counselling approaches to supervision will be found in Edgar Stones' *Supervision in Teacher Education* (1984) and Gunnar Handal and Per Lauvas *Promoting Reflective Teaching: Supervision in Action* (1987).

For a very clear introduction to the details of a variety of observation techniques, Ann Malamah-Thomas *Classroom Interaction* (1987) can be recommended. Dick Allwright's *Observation in the Language Class-*

room (1988) should be read, not only for the writer's own insights, based on many years of researching into classroom observation, but also for the access it provides to original writings from other key writers – Moskowitz and Fanselow, for example.

Next, there are a few titles relating to teaching and learning in higher education. The first is Noel Entwistle *Styles of Learning and Teaching* (1981), a very readable account of topics in educational psychology which are highly relevant to tertiary education (and indeed to other levels of education as well). The second is R. Beard and J. Hartley *Teaching and Learning in Higher Education*. This is an authoritative survey which has been regularly updated: the references in the present book are to the fourth edition (1984). A useful, reasoned 'how-to-do-it' book is G. Brown and M. Atkins *Effective Teaching in Higher Education* (1988). On group work, the comprehensive account by D. Jaques *Learning in Groups* (1984) can be highly recommended.

Finally, to round off this highly selective list, there is the excellent book on course design in higher education by Derek Rowntree *Developing Courses for Students* (second edition 1985). It also has very useful chapters on assessment and evaluation.

Bibliography

Allwright, D. (1988). *Observation in the Language Classroom*. London: Longman.

Andrews, R. (1971). *Microteaching Methods: A Critique*. ULIE Bulletin No. 23. London: University of London, Institute of Education.

Atkin, J.M. (1968). Research styles in science education. *Journal of Research in Science Teaching*, 5, 338–45.

Ausubel, D.P. (1965). Cognitive structure and the facilitation of meaningful verbal learning. In R.C. Anderson and D.P. Ausubel (eds.), *Readings in the Psychology of Cognition*. New York: Holt, Rinehart and Winston.

Barnett, R.A., Becher, R.A. & Cork, N.M. (1987). Models of professional preparation: pharmacy, nursing and teacher education. *Studies in Higher Education*, 12, 1, 51–63.

Bartley, D.E. (1969). Microteaching: rationale, procedures and application to foreign language. *Audio-Visual Language Journal*, 7, 3, 139–44.

Bassey, M. (1986). Does action research require sophisticated research methods? In D. Hustler, T. Cassidy & T. Cuff (eds.), *Action Research in Classrooms and Schools*. London: Allen and Unwin.

Beard, R. & Hartley, J. (1984). *Teaching and Learning in Higher Education* (4th ed.). London: Harper and Row.

Bellack, A.A., Kliebard, H.M., Hyman, R.T. & Smith, F.L. (1966). *The Language of the Classroom*. New York: Teachers College Press, Columbia University.

Bligh, D.A. (1971). *What's the Use of Lectures?* Harmondsworth, England: Penguin Books.

Borg, W.R., Kelly, M.L., Langer, P. & Gall, M. (1970). *The Minicourse: A Microteaching Approach to Teacher Education*. London: Collier-Macmillan.

Borich, G.D. & Madden, S.K. (1977). *Evaluating Classroom Instruction: A Source Book of Instruments*. Reading, Massachusetts: Addison-Wesley.

Boud, D., Keogh, R. & Walker, D. (eds.) (1985). *Reflection – Turning Experience into Learning*. London: Kogan Page; New York: Nichols Publishing Company.

Bowers, R.G. (1980a). *Verbal Behaviour in the Language Teaching Classroom*. Reading, England: Ph.D Thesis, University of Reading.

Bowers, R.G. (1980*b*). How effective are efficient teachers? (Paper presented at the International Colloquium on Classroom Interaction. Paris, 1980. Published in 1982 by Goethe Institute, Munich, in the *Pariser Werkstattgesprache* series.)

Bowers, R. (1987). Developing perceptions of the classroom. In R. Bowers (ed.), *Language Teacher Education: An Integrated Programme for ELT Teacher Training.* ELT Documents. Oxford: Pergamon Press / Modern English Publications.

Bramley, W. (1979). *Group Tutoring: Concepts and Case Studies.* London: Kogan Page.

Bright, J.A. (1968). The training of teachers of English as a second language in Africa. In G.E. Perren (ed.), *Teachers of English as a Second Language: Their Training and Preparation.* Cambridge: Cambridge University Press.

Britten, D. (1985). Teacher Training in ELT. *Language Teaching Abstracts,* **18**, 2/3.

Brown, G. & Atkins, M. (1988). *Effective Teaching in Higher Education.* London and New York: Methuen.

Brown, R. (1988). Classroom pedagogics: a syllabus for the interactive stage? *The Teacher Trainer,* **2**, 3, 13–17; **2**, 4, 8–9.

Bruner, J.S. (1965). The act of discovery. In R.C. Anderson & D.P. Ausubel (eds.), *Readings in the Psychology of Cognition.* New York: Holt, Rinehart and Winston.

Clarke, M.A. (1983). The scope of approach, the importance of method, and the nature of technique. In J.E. Alatis, H.E. Stern & P. Stevens (eds.), *Applied Linguistics and the Preparation of Second Language Teachers: Toward a Rationale (GURT 1983).* Washington, DC: Georgetown University Press.

Cogan, M.L. (1973). *Clinical Supervision.* Boston: Houghton Mifflin.

Copeland, W.D. (1982). Student teachers' preference for supervisory approach. *Journal of Teacher Education,* **33**, 2, 32–6.

Coulthard, M. (1977). *An Introduction to Discourse Analysis.* London: Longman.

Cousin, W.D., Carver, D.J., Dodgson, C.F. & Petrie, J.K.F. (1978). Prescriptive categories in microteaching in a pre-service TEFL programme. *System,* **6**, 2, 98–105.

Cripwell, K. (1979). Microteaching in the training of teachers of English as a second or foreign language. In K. Cripwell & M. Geddes (eds.), *Microteaching and EFL Teacher Training.* London: University of London Institute of Education.

Croll, P. (1986). *Systematic Classroom Observation.* London: The Falmer Press.

Curran, C.A. (1978). *Understanding: A Necessary Ingredient in Human Belonging.* East Dubuque, Illinois: Counseling-Learning Publications.

Doff, A. (1988). *Teach English: A training course for teachers.* Cambridge: Cambridge University Press.

Dunkin, M.J. & Biddle, B.J. (1974). *The Study of Teaching.* Lanham/ New York/London: University Press of America.

Edge, J. (1988). Training, Education, Development: Worlds Apart? (Paper given at the Annual Conference of the British Association for Teaching and Research in Overseas Education, Moray House College, Edinburgh).

Elbaz, F. (1983). *Teacher Thinking: A Study of Practical Knowledge.* London: Croom Helm.

Ellis, G. & Sinclair, B. (1989). *Learning to Learn English: A Course in Learner Training.* Cambridge: Cambridge University Press.

Entwistle, N. & Wilson, J.D. (1977). *Degrees of Excellence: The Academic Achievement Game.* London: Hodder & Stoughton.

Entwistle, N. (1981). *Styles of Learning and Teaching: An Integrated Outline of Educational Psychology for Students, Teachers and Lecturers.* Chichester, England: John Wiley.

Fanselow, J.F. (1977). Beyond RASHOMON – conceptualising and describing the teaching act. *TESOL Quarterly,* **11**, 1, 17–32.

Fanselow, J.F. (1987). *Breaking Rules: Generating and Exploring Alternatives in Language Teaching.* New York and London: Longman.

Flanders, N.A. (1970). *Analyzing Teacher Behavior.* Reading, Massachusetts: Addison-Wesley.

Freeman, D. (1982). Observing teachers: three approaches to in-service training and development. *TESOL Quarterly,* **16**, 1, 21–28.

Furlong, V.J., Hirst, P.H., Pocklington, K. & Miles, S. (1988). *Initial Teacher Training and the Role of the School.* Milton Keynes, England: Open University Press.

Gebhard, J.C. (1984). Models of supervision: choices. *TESOL Quarterly,* **18**, 3, 501–14.

Geddes, M. & Raz, H. (1979). Studying pupil-teacher interaction. In S. Holden (ed.), *Teacher Training.* London: Modern English Publications.

Gibbs, G. (1981). *Teaching Students to Learn: A Student-Centred Approach.* Milton Keynes, England: Open University Press.

Gibbs, G., Habeshaw, S. & Habeshaw, T. (1987). *53 Interesting Things to do in your Lectures* (2nd ed.). Bristol: Technical and Educational Services.

Goldhammer, R. (1969). *Clinical Supervision: Special Methods for the Supervision of Teachers.* New York: Holt, Rinehart and Winston. (Note: a revised version of this book is also available: Goldhammer, R., Anderson, R.H. & Krajewski, R. (1980). *Clinical Supervision: Special Methods for the Supervision of Teachers* (2nd ed.). New York: Holt, Rinehart and Winston.)

Greene, J. (1986). *Language Understanding: A Cognitive Approach.* Milton Keynes, England: Open University Press.

Gregory, T.B. (1972). *Encounters with Teaching.* Englewood Cliffs, New Jersey: Prentice-Hall.

Halliday, M.A.K. & Hasan, R. (1976). *Cohesion in English.* London: Longman.

Hammersley, M. & Atkinson, P. (1983). *Ethnography: Principles in Practice.* London and New York: Tavistock Publications.

Handal, G. & Lauvas, P. (1987). *Promoting Reflective Teaching: Supervision in Action.* Milton Keynes: SRHE / Open University Press.

Hart, W.A. (1978). Against Skills. *Oxford Review of Education*, 4, 2, 205–16.

Heath, R. (1964). *The Reasonable Adventurer.* Pittsburgh: University of Pittsburgh Press.

Heath, R. (1978). Personality and the development of students in higher education. In C.A. Parker (ed.), *Encouraging Development in College Students.* Minneapolis: University of Minnesota Press.

Hopkins, D. (1985). *A Teacher's Guide to Classroom Research.* Milton Keynes, England: Open University Press.

Hudson, L. (1968). *Frames of Mind.* London: Methuen.

Hustler, D., Cassidy, T. & Cuff, T. (eds.) (1986). *Action Research in Classrooms and Schools.* London: Allen and Unwin.

Jaques, D. (1984). *Learning in Groups.* London: Croom Helm.

Johnstone, R. (1977). Microteaching and Modern Languages. In D. McIntyre, G. MacLeod & R. Griffiths (eds.), *Investigations of Microteaching.* London: Croom Helm.

Kerry, T. (series ed.) (1981). *DES Teacher Education Project Focus Books.* London: Macmillan.

Knights, S. (1985). Reflection and learning: the importance of a listener. In D. Boud, R. Keogh & D. Walker (eds.), *Reflection – Turning Experience into Learning.* London: Kogan Page; New York: Nichols Publishing Company.

Lawless, C.J. (1971). Microteaching without hardware: developments at the University of Malawi. *Teacher Education in New Countries*, 12, 53–63.

McGarvey, B. and Swallow, D. (1986). *Microteaching in Teacher Education and Training.* London: Croom Helm.

McIntyre, D. (1977). Microteaching practice, collaboration with peers and supervisory feedback as determinants of the effects of microteaching. In D. McIntyre, G. MacLeod & R. Griffiths (eds.), *Investigations of Microteaching.* London: Croom Helm.

McIntyre, D. (1988). Designing a teacher education curriculum from research and theory on teacher knowledge. In J. Calderhead (ed.), *Exploring Teachers' Thinking.* London: Cassell.

MacLeod, G. & McIntyre, D. (1977). Towards a model for microteaching. In D. McIntyre, G. MacLeod & R. Griffiths (eds.), *Investigations of Microteaching*. London: Croom Helm.

McKnight, P.C. (1971). Microteaching in Teacher Training. *Research in Education*, 6, 24–38.

Main, A. (1980). *Encouraging Effective Learning*. Edinburgh: Scottish Academic Press.

Malamah-Thomas, A. (1987). *Classroom Interaction*. Oxford: Oxford University Press.

Marris, P. (1964). *The Experience of Higher Education*. London: Routledge and Kegan Paul.

Miller, C. & Parlett, M.R. (1974). *Up to the Mark: A Study of the Examination Game*. London: Society for Research in Higher Education.

Mitchell, R. & Parkinson, B. (1979). A systematic linguistic analysis of the strategies of foreign language teaching in the secondary school. BAAL Conference Paper: Mimeo.

Moskowitz, G. (1968). The effects of training foreign language teachers in interaction analysis. *Foreign Language Annals*, 1, 3, 218–35.

Moskowitz, G. (1971). Interaction analysis: a new modern language for supervisors. *Foreign Language Annals*, 5, 2, 211–21.

Moskowitz, G. (1978). *Caring and Sharing in the Foreign Language Class: A Source Book on Humanistic Techniques*. New York: Newbury House.

Parker, J.C. & Rubin, L.J. (1966). *Process as Content: Curriculum Design and the Application of Knowledge*. Chicago: Rand McNally.

Parlett, M.R. (1970). The syllabus-bound student. In L. Hudson (ed.), *The Ecology of Human Intelligence*. Harmondsworth, England: Penguin Books.

Pask, G. & Scott, B.C.E. (1972). Learning strategies and individual competence. *International Journal of Man-Machine Studies*, 4, 217–53.

Perlberg, A. & Theodor, E. (1975). Patterns and styles in the supervision of teachers. *British Journal of Teacher Education*, 1, 203–11.

Perrott, E. (1982). *Effective Teaching: A Practical Guide to Improving Your Teaching*. London: Longman.

Politzer, R. (1970). Some reflections on 'Good' and 'Bad' language teaching behaviors. *Language Learning*, 20, 2, 31–43.

Ramani, E. (1987). Theorizing from the Classroom. *ELT Journal*, 41, 1, 3–11.

Retallick, H. (1986). Clinical supervision: technical collaborative and critical approaches. In W.J. Smyth (ed.), *Learning about Teaching through Clinical Supervision*. London: Croom Helm.

Rowntree, D. (1985). *Developing Courses for Students*. London: Paul Chapman.

Schön, D.A. (1983). *The Reflective Practitioner: How Professionals Think in Action.* London: Temple Smith.

Schön, D.A. (1987). *Educating the Reflective Practitioner: Toward a New Design for Teaching and Learning in the Professions.* San Francisco: Jossey Bass.

Sergiovanni, T.J. (1977). Reforming teacher evaluation: naturalistic alternatives. *Education Leadership.* 34, 8, 602–7.

Sergiovanni, T.J. & Starratt, R.J. (1983). *Supervision: Human Perspectives* (3rd ed.). New York: McGraw-Hill.

Sinclair, J. McH. & Coulthard, R.M. (1975). *Towards an Analysis of Discourse.* Oxford: Oxford University Press.

Smyth, W.J. (1986). Towards a collaborative, reflective and critical mode of clinical supervision. In W.J. Smyth (ed.), *Learning about Teaching through Clinical Supervision.* London: Croom Helm.

Stenhouse, L. (1975). *An Introduction to Curriculum Research and Development.* London: Heinemann.

Stoddart, J. (1981). *Microteaching: Current Practice in Britain with Special Reference to ESOL.* London: University of London, Institute of Education.

Stones, E. & Morris, S. (1972). *Teaching Practice: Problems and Perspectives.* London: Methuen.

Stones, E. (1984). *Supervision in Teacher Education.* London: Methuen.

Stubbs, M. & Delamont, S. (1976). *Exploration in Classroom Observation.* Chichester, England: John Wiley.

Tomalin, B. (1988). Video and Teacher Education. Paper given at 22nd International Conference IATEFL/TESOL Scotland, Edinburgh, April 1988.

Turney, C., Clift, J.C., Dunkin, M.J. & Traill, R.D. (1973). *Microteaching: Research, Theory and Practice.* Sydney: Sydney University Press.

Walker, D. (1985). Writing and Reflection. In D. Boud, R. Keogh & D. Walker (eds.), *Reflection – Turning Experience into Learning.* London: Kogan Page; New York: Nichols Publishing Company.

Walker, R. (1985). *Doing Research: A Handbook for Teachers.* London: Methuen.

Wallace, M.J. (1979). Microteaching. In S. Holden (ed.), *Teacher Training.* London: Modern English Publications.

Wallace, M.J. (1981*a*). Microteaching without hardware in Argentina. In D. Carver and M.J. Wallace (eds.), *SCEO Microteaching Papers.* Edinburgh: Scottish Centre for Education Overseas, Moray House College.

Wallace, M.J. (1981*b*). Toward a skill-based analysis of EFL teaching skills. *TESOL Quarterly,* 15, 2, 151–7.

Wallace, M.J. (1982). Individualisation in Study Skills. (Paper given at a seminar on Individualism in Language Learning, University of Manchester).

Wallace, M.J. (1988). The case for a key-stage observation schedule as a training device in TESOL teacher education. Paper given at 6th Annual TESOL Scotland Conference, Edinburgh, November 1988.

Ward, B.E. (1970). *A Survey of Microteaching in NCATE – Accredited Secondary Education Programs.* Stanford, California: Stanford University School of Education.

Weller, R.H. (1971). *Verbal Communication in Instructional Supervision.* New York: Teachers College Press, Columbia University.

Witkin, H.A., Moore, C.A., Goodenough, D.R. & Cox, P.W. (1977). Field-dependent and field-independent cognitive styles and their educational implications. *Review of Educational Research*, 47, 1, 1–64.

Wragg, E.C. (1974). *Teaching teaching.* Newton Abbot, England: David and Charles.

Zeichner, K.M. & Liston, D.P. (1985). Teaching student teachers to reflect. *Harvard Educational Review*, 57, 1, 23–48.

Index

Printed in the United Kingdom
by Lightning Source UK Ltd.
104953UKS00001B/172-174